T0365654

WHY GOD

WILLIAM J. PARDUE

WestBow
PRESS
A DIVISION OF THOMAS NELSON

WestBow Press books may be ordered through booksellers or by contacting:

WestBow Press
A Division of Thomas Nelson
1663 Liberty Drive
Bloomington, IN 47403
www.westbowpress.com
1-(866) 928-1240

Because of the dynamic nature of the Internet, any web addresses or links contained in this book may have changed since publication and may no longer be valid. The views expressed in this work are solely those of the author and do not necessarily reflect the views of the publisher, and the publisher hereby disclaims any responsibility for them.

Any people depicted in stock imagery provided by Thinkstock are models, and such images are being used for illustrative purposes only.

Certain stock imagery © Thinkstock.

ISBN: 978-1-4497-4787-9 (sc)

Library of Congress Control Number: 2012906730

Printed in the United States of America

WestBow Press rev. date: 05/08/2012

TABLE OF CONTENTS

PART I

THREADS OF PROOF

PART TWO

THE LINE OF TIME

PART I

THREADS OF PROOF

WHY GOD

If you gain, you gain all; if you lose, you lose nothing. Wager then without hesitation, that He exists.

Blaise Pascal (1623-1662)
French mathematician, physicist and philosopher

Why God? This question is asking for an explanation of why anyone should take God seriously. It is a question for our times as it seems the old God as we came to know him has disappointed. If he exists does he really have anything relevant to say to us today or is his time past. Are there any cosmic imperatives which we are subject to when it comes to a God concept? Is there a real God who is relevant, helpful and loving who can be contacted by us all and in that contact has the power to transform?

The answers to these questions is what this book intends to explore. You may be discomfited, perhaps insulted by some of what is written in these pages. At various times you will be forced to confront your beliefs about important matters in your spiritual life. I will forewarn you that on some pages you will have no place to hide. It is at that point that you may take the blindfold off and see the rest of the world. My hope is that when you finish the last page you will be left with important questions about yourself, the cosmos and God which you will carry with you until you find the answers for yourself. The aim is to incite a flame of curiosity about the greatest question ever put to mankind. Is there really a God? Is it all myth and if not what is the foundation for believing that a God exists? Why should any non-believer suddenly pick up the yoke of faith and deviate from a path of total self indulgence?

I am convinced that this is the most important question facing the human species today. The answer to the question will determine if our species can continue to survive. Man is not just a physical being. He is also a spiritual being. Our idea of what constitutes spiritual may differ but man's drift away from his spiritual self has had disastrous consequences for us on the material level. We can't trust anyone and we are at War with someone, somewhere at all times. Our political system is infected by the human virus commonly referred to as greed, pride and self dealing. Our religious institutions are infected with the same virus. In fact all the institutions which we use to put our trust in are no longer trustworthy because the people, or at least a significant number of them, who lead these institutions are grounded in their physical selves with no idea of how evil and decadent they have become. Our common goal has now become the quest for king of the hill regardless of whom it is that must be sacrificed in the process.

Consider the country's current financial and moral crisis. Millions of Americans have suffered losses of their entire assets and income. They have lost their homes, their jobs and many have taken their lives leaving their families to struggle on. Now this state of affairs was caused by individuals in corporations, banks, real estate concerns, investment houses and insurance companies whose only concern was adding to their bank accounts. They did not then and they do not now even blink an eye at the tragedy and human misery which their greed created. They sense no connection to the unfortunate people who were not clever enough to avoid the crash.

The chief benefit of the spiritual life is that it teaches and demonstrates the unbreakable connection between all people. It underlines the fact that your act, your thought may not come back to you today but it will return and you will either be pleased to welcome it home or you will be dreading the very thought of having to answer to your creation in your own life. It is a life of compassion. It is a life of peace, tranquility and beneficence.

Because our lives move at such a fast pace these days it is difficult to see the connection between that thought or action which was ours and its consequences in our lives when the two do not immediately follow one after the other. Besides we see "bad people", people who have committed acts that have harmed other people, who prosper and seem to walk away unscathed from the human misery which they have created. It is perhaps more disturbing that we admire these people as the supreme providers. They are the top of the food chain, taking what they want without any regard for the short term consequences to others and the long term consequences to themselves. They pride themselves on their conquests, their acquisitions above all else.

We are a society in which we all suffer from Attention Deficit Disorder. When is the last time you had a conversation with someone who was either only pretending to listen, texting on their phone, or talking so relentlessly that you could have fallen asleep and they would not have noticed nor would they have stopped talking. The problem with this condition is that the spiritual world operates at a different pace, a much slower pace. It requires a lack of impatience, anxiety and preoccupation to make contact. It is everywhere but you cannot make contact with it unless you slow down and listen for it, watch for it, feel it, breathe it, smell it, taste it and live it.

The spiritual world proceeds at an organic growth rate and it has seasons. The physical world proceeds at the 4G rate, an eighty miles per hour rate, winning a million dollars in one hour on television rate, erasing wrinkles in a one minute commercial rate, and instantaneously communicating with someone on the other side of the world rate. It does not recognize night and day and it has no seasons. Technology is incredible and it has provided an abundance of benefits to the human race. It has also dissembled man's sense of himself and created false selves that we pursue while our souls whither on the vine and today's prophets are trolling for more friends on facebook. We are no longer what our mighty species used to be, back in the day when the world was equally ruled by the spiritual and the material, a balanced partnership. Those were gritty but truly miraculous times, when men wondered at the stars and reverenced their mystical existence. They felt life flowing through them and it burned their souls with its magnificence. If we are the plastic palm tree in the lobby of the Holiday Inn in L.A. then they were the Giant Redwoods which towers above all its neighbors, reaching toward the heavens while protecting the life living beneath its limbs. Just listen to the names, Joshua, Moses, Abraham, Mohammed, Jesus, Osiris, Buddha, Confucius, Solomon, and Socrates, read what they had to say and how they said it. Those were times when men who acted like Gods and perhaps some who were Gods walked this earth, spoke to the people and delivered their messages in person while looking you in the eye. They left us behind and the evolution of our "personal resurrection towards enlightenment" has sputtered. There were not cell phones to distract the listener from the message, no televisions capturing their attention while Buddha spoke to his followers of his revelations.

We as a species must change our ways or perish. We already see the disaster in the wind if we do not adjust our behaviors and our attitudes towards our planet and our fellow brothers and sisters who inhabit this planet with us we are doomed.

WHY ME NOW

The short answer to that question is because it is the divine will. The other short answer is because I had a life crisis and I found that God, the divine spirit, the cosmic force, could actually help me. There are many people who know me who would have a good laugh if they knew I had even considered writing on this topic. Until a year and one half ago I had not been inside a church or considered the question of God for forty years. Please know that when I use the word God in these pages it is includes any name which you would like to give to that force which is present in our everyday lives and can be contacted. Additionally it has the characteristics of compassion, unconditional love, acceptance, forgiveness and beneficence among others.

The concept of God has been around forever and has arisen in countless forms and characters. There have always been true believers who have in the most extreme circumstances of persecution for their beliefs given their lives for God. They have been torn asunder by wild animals, crucified, burned at the stake, stoned, drowned, buried alive, impaled, skinned, roasted and killed in every conceivable manner which man's cruelty could devise. All of this blood-letting, death and torture could simply have been avoided by a public denial of their God. Of course not all followers held fast to their beliefs in the face of the certainty of a horrible and brutal death but some did. I heard a very interesting fact recently concerning those persecuted and put to death because of their belief in God. It seems that there have been more Christians killed for their faith in the last one hundred years that any other time in recorded history. I wouldn't have guessed that but back to the ancient martyrs.

We are not interested in those that relinquished their faith when faced with the above options. The only ones who matter for the purposes of this book are those who held fast and did not waiver from their belief in a higher power, a cosmic entity who or which created and controls everything. It is not necessary to even know their names or circumstances of their lives because the only important piece of evidence is that they existed and held an idea to be of such value and importance that it was worth suffering any hardship, enduring any pain, relinquishing any possession including family. They valued this idea of a God above anything else in their world. Their personal relationship with God surpassed any earthly pleasure or love which they had experienced. They were beyond faith. They knew God intimately, personally and loved him above all else. Without this personal knowledge of a supreme being they would have succumbed to the torture which they faced and recanted their faith in their God.

This is a piece of real evidence, historical evidence, objective evidence which cannot be ignored when we ask the question, why God? God's detractors will likely posit that such a belief is crazy, irrational, and held only by individuals who are easily influenced and conned by the Priests, prophets and disciples. The weak minded can always be duped. There is a fool born every minute. On the face of it that argument has some merit when analyzed rationally, subjected to the scientific scrutiny and rational deism which currently reigns supreme over the human race.

A belief in God is, as is a belief in anything, a choice made by an individual. Whatever the mental construct is by which you navigate your life you can rest assured that you have chosen to believe it to be true. Free will is a marvelous and powerful mental dynamic which was either given to us by God or evolved through the ages as a useful tool in the survival of our species. It allows us to choose to believe in a higher power and act on that belief or to not believe and as a consequence not take actions which would express that belief. Of course those who believe in rationalism have also chosen their God to the exclusion of all others.

This book puts the God concept to the test. It examines evidence and draws conclusions from that evidence. It is not biblical evidence which we will examine but evidence which exists in our day to day lives. Evidence which either leads us towards the idea of a God or away from it to some Cosmic String Theory or Quantum Physics which represent the other Gods which we have created to give us a sense of being in control of our destinies. It is our own attempt at usurping and replacing a sense of any cosmic force which presumes to be greater than man.

As a clarification, God for the purposes of this book has no particular religious affiliation, gender, race, ethnicity, political affiliation, or favorite football team. God if he exists is all of life. He was here before us and will be here after us. He created everything which we see and that we cannot see. We are his progeny, his creation and we along with all other life forms come from him. If he or some other omniscient force does not exist to determine the direction of life and therefore give it some substantive meaning then all of life is inconsequential, a mere anomaly.

The existence of a God gives life a special place in the cosmic mix because any God whom we can imagine always favors man as the only apparent creature who can know him and therefore worship him. God it appears needs man to complete his plan. It is essential to remember that if a God does exist he is incapable of being defined by any religion, philosophy, dogma or other mode of capturing his essence. Furthermore he is not the "religion or dogma" that attempts to contain him within their creed. He is beyond that as well as part of all that. He cannot be explained. He can only be experienced. He is not the map he is the destination.

WHY OPEN THE DOOR

I stood in the restaurant bathroom, alone, sweating, panic barely under control and I felt the fear take control. My family waited in the restaurant for their meals unaware of the state of terror which I had entered. I couldn't let anyone know that I was shaken to the core with doubt, anxiety, depression and a complete sense of panic. The feeling had grown over the last month as events in my life came together to form the perfect storm which threatened to consume me.

If you have never been to that place where you are completely alone and all the tools and skills which you have honed over a lifetime are powerless to rescue you then consider yourself fortunate. It is a life altering moment. It is a moment which sucks the life out of you and with it your will to continue. You find yourself wondering how you had managed to succeed for so long and avoid this moment of truth. You look in the mirror in that bathroom and you do not recognize the image returning your gaze. You are a lost child stumbling through the dark forest with the sound of the wolves or better yet the Lion reverberating through your being, snapping at your heels. Your cries go unheeded. There is no mother or father to rescue you for they are long past. There is no friend, spouse, or family member who can fathom the depth of your despair. You find a level place on the cold forest floor to lie down and sobbing you wait for the end as fear creeps over you. It squeezes your heart in an iron grip and twists your stomach in knots. It tears at your very soul. It is Satan's finest moment. He has his hand wrapped tightly around your soul squeezing the life out of it.

It is the moment when all of your self-doubts meet in a crescendo of pent up anxieties that deafen you to any other sound. You only hear your own insecurities, doubts, mistakes, errors, weaknesses, and addictions and know yourself to be evil. The Devil is applauding the results of his efforts. He is ecstatic.

It is the beginning of the dissembling of the persona which you have created to explain who you are to the world. In that moment when you glimpse your true self it is as if you have moved from the Penthouse apartment to the park bench. You woke up in the Park, ragged, dirty, and reeking of your own urine and you have no idea how you got there but you are devastated. You want to find a place to hide. You wonder how long you have been like this and who has noticed. You already know the answer to that because everyone else has seen that ragged man on the park bench except you. It is at this precise moment that we hear a knocking. It is familiar but you can't place it but you feel compelled to take heed and open the door for the first time in your life. God smiles at you and looks at you with only love. He says welcome home and you just want to cry.

It was in this time of complete and utter desolation that I made the decision to try a belief in God. I don't mean that

I suddenly was born again but that I consciously searched for help and I found references to God almost everywhere I looked. I had never purchased a book on God before but suddenly every book which I purchased had references to God. I was literally not interested in any other topic other than one that explained God to me. This was more than coincidence; this was the cosmic force directing me, moving me to where I needed to be. It wasn't the first time in my life I had experienced this guidance. It had happened before I just had not assigned the credit to a God with whom I could communicate in real time.

I moved hesitantly toward God. I did not want to let anyone see me buying those kinds of books. But I was compelled to at least explore the possibility of an all powerful entity that actually cared about my dilemma and cared enough to help me with my problems if I just asked for help. Of course I was not about to tell anyone that I had even considered a return to spirituality or God. I was too proud and too educated to ever consider the God myth to be real. I could not admit my search to anyone because I did not want to be thought the fool; however, a force moved me to open my mind enough to privately explore the possibility of his existence. I must admit that I was also intellectually challenged by the idea that avoiding God and failing to take the subject matter seriously even for the distinct purpose of social experimentation was being narrow minded and ignorant. Ignorant in the sense of someone who believes they know the answer to some question when they have only formed an opinion without ever carefully examining the subject matter with an intellectual freedom and complete lack of fear in being discovered entertaining such an idea.

It is interesting to note that to examine the idea of God in our culture requires courage. It is not a serious subject among the self styled intellectuals. There is a distinct arrogance which reigns supreme and pours its condescension over you when it is discovered that you have religious leanings. You are tuned out, not taken seriously, referred to as a religious nut case.

I look back now at that moment in the restroom, bending over the sink, gasping for air, sweating profusely while feeling completely and utterly lost down to the very center of my being. In that moment I saw myself for who I was, not who I imagined myself to be. It was a reality check of cosmic importance. I peeked through the curtain of my delusions and caught a glimpse of some dark and sinister stranger who hid in the shadows of my ego and laughed at my lack of insight into my own persona. The person whom I had created, who I had introduced to those who I knew was a fiction. The reality of who I was deflated my rational world and hurled me into a season of "a dark night of the soul". I not only saw but felt my arrogance, callousness, selfishness and pride. It was painful. It was a living nightmare.

I recount this experience because it drove me to the idea of God. I needed help. I had no one else to turn to. I didn't know anyone who I believed was capable of giving me help except someone as loving, forgiving, wise, powerful and accessible as God was described as being. The other key characteristic which God offered was his accessibility and complete discretion. If he truly existed I could count on him to not tell anyone else what I may have to confess to him. That was the point that closed the deal for me. I was also drawn to the image and character of a shepherd or father who had nothing but the best interests of his flock and his children in mind. He loved them equally and unconditionally. This was a comforting and soothing thought.

The culture I was raised in did not suffer weakness from men. Weakness of mind or of body was considered unmanly, despicable. Even if you were falling apart you held it together for all to admire your strength and courage. As a result of this cultural vaccination against self revelation I was not permitted to show weakness or to fail. God, however, was the exception for it became apparent to me that he accepted all sheep back to the fold and all children back home without any recriminations.

One of the ideas which I became attached to immediately upon being introduced to it was that God was always knocking on our door waiting for us to open it. That idea intrigued me. God was attempting to contact me and had been for quite some time. I considered whether that might be true by reviewing my life and any hints that God was knocking and I was just too dumb or deaf to try to figure out what in the world that noise was. We are only capable of hearing God knocking when all other distractions become insignificant as our survival mechanisms kick into action in our moment of crisis. He who seeks him shall find him.

THE FIRST DREAM,
THE FLOODED CATHEDRAL

I have always been intensely interested in dreams and have since I was young attempted to remember them and meditate on those that I could recall. During this religious revival period I began to experience a progressive series of dreams with a religious significance. I have learned through the years that dreams often attempt to communicate messages to us especially during difficult times in our lives. They provide us answers which we are incapable of obtaining in the waking state. During this period this entity or force which we call God was communicating with me through my dreams. He was not only knocking on my door but when I opened the door he wanted to talk but I he didn't use words, as words are unable to communicate an idea as big as God. Instead of words God showed me dream pictures. It is the old saying that a picture is worth a thousand words and it was clear that God understands that concept thoroughly.

The first in this series of dreams was in this beginning period of my exploration of the God concept and its possibility as a lifeboat for me.

I was standing on a cliff overlooking the ocean and immediately below me I saw a Cathedral submerged along the shoreline to the bottom of the dome which was the highest point of the Church. The water was clear along the shore and I could see the wavy outline of the rest of the structure below the water. The dome was capped by a crucifix both of which stood above the level of the sea. The entire structure was intact and in surprisingly good shape. My first thought was that it only needed to be raised out of the sea onto land. It belonged on the land where it would be accessible, where it could be utilized by believers. My second thought was that I should move it from its location to the highest point on land.

God was right. I had abandoned my ties to religion and yet they still remained accessible for rehabilitation. I just had to put some effort into the relocation so that it occupied a site where it would be more accessible, more useful for my purposes. That Cathedral had been waiting for me for forty years, just waiting, knowing that I would eventually rediscover a potential for faith in something other than my own abilities, my own self. That structure represented a nescient belief in God, an abiding yearning for some higher power that I could count on to rescue me if I ever needed it. God was letting me know that my faith in him had always been there and was now ready for a resurrection.

At this point in my life I had not attended Church since I was a freshman in college forty three years before. I was raised a Catholic and had been indoctrinated into the faith with all its rites, rituals and statuary but I had walked away at age seventeen. Until this period of crisis I had not thought much about organized religion which was positive. It was time to put aside the preconceived ideas I had when I was a teenager and approach God without the bias which I had as a young man.

When I left it the Church was a greedy sacrilege which had nothing to do with God and everything to do with money and dogma. The God of that church did not exist for the regular folk and only the priests could communicate with him. That was not the God I needed at this point in my life. It was not the God that I needed at any point in my life. A confessional manned by a priest who knew nothing of my pain was totally useless. I needed a dose of the real thing if there was such a thing. I was bound and determined to raise that Church from the waters and move it to high ground. God could not have been clearer in his indictment of my discarded faith. I wanted to walk through the doors of that Church and have God greet me and talk to me.

The Church dream was my first message from him and it was beyond perfect. My problem became communicating back. The books I read suggested prayer. The only praying I had ever done was a mindless and mechanical recitation of Hail Mary's or Our Father's after repeating the same confession that I had repeated for most of my youth. This was not praying. This was a monstrous demonization of prayer. There was no life to it no vibrancy, no meaning. It had no ability to move or transform you. The advice which I received was to treat prayer as a confession to God of what was ailing you. Ask him for guidance and wait for the answer.

It was awkward at first because I just repeated the same prayer which I had memorized night after night. The importance of that time was not what I said but that it was a beginning of me saying anything at all to God. It was a movement towards God not away from him. I had been moving away from him for many years. Prayer, I learned was how one communicated with God, nothing more and nothing less. He had been waiting for me to call him.

I learned in my readings that prayer was transformative. It was suggested that it was the perfect act because when you prayed it transformed you. They were right. Something about the act of acknowledging the possibility of a higher power and asking that higher power for help was transformative. It changed how you thought about things and what things you thought about. It removed you from the center of the universe and allowed a consideration that you may not wield the ultimate power in your life. It allowed you the possibility that there just might be a greater power than what was contained between your ears which was directing cosmic forces.

Another quote which deeply impressed me at the time was "no matter how many steps you have taken away from God it is always only one step back to him." It was true. I took one step back towards him and he was there guiding me and picking up the pieces. After forty years of ignoring him, worshiping false idols, not worshiping any idols except myself, and just having a scorched earth policy as I blazed a trail to my various goals he was there, just waiting patiently for my return. Perhaps this is the answer that I have been looking for in so many wrong places.

This idea of communicating with God through prayer was powerful. It not only soothed me to know I could tell him anything, ask him anything, ask for anything and he never failed to respond. Every time I needed something, desperately needed something and I prayed he answered me. Although my learned skepticism kept me from shouting on the street corners in tongues I was secretly surprised and amazed at the results of my efforts to communicate with whomever it was that was paying attention to me. I could not believe that the God I had been so diligently searching for in so many different religions was always right there looking over my shoulder wondering where I was looking for him now. He was real and he was responsive. I was not totally convinced. Perhaps it was just coincidence but I had nothing else.

I prayed every night and every day. I prayed driving my car and I learned to communicate more clearly and more sincerely. I never told anyone that I was praying because it felt so strange, so bizarre that I was actually praying to God on a daily basis. It is indeed a very strange world in a wonderful sort of way.

As I embarked on this spiritual exploration I was guided by an unknown entity. I learned several things early on in my journey. Perhaps the most important was that I had been searching for God by sorting through religious dogma. I was looking for him there, in a place where he never was. I have learned that if there is truly a God he is only accessible in the present moment. There is an incredible amount of hearsay evidence about God but the real God the one that moves you is in the moment. You can feel him working in you. You experience the peace and lessening of anxiety which he brings to your life. You live the transformation and at each step you have the choice of continuing in the same direction or abandoning the search. A taste of God, however, can be very addictive. It slowly envelopes you and the most important thing in your life becomes getting closer to the source.

I also discovered that God cannot be approached through reason. He cannot be communicated with or understood through any linear, rationalistic, diagnostic methodology. Religion can be approached and torn apart with these methods but not God. He can only be understood in a visceral, intuitive, holistic way. God is too big, too comprehensive, too complex for our crude reasoning to comprehend. He can only be felt and experienced. While science and mathematics can be learned en masse and the understanding tested with objective tests, the understanding of God cannot be tested in such a manner. You know him when you feel him there is no other way.

Assuming that a specific religion is the same as God is a gross misconception. Just as looking at a map of Italy is not being in Italy the Bible is not God. It is easy to attack the irrationality in the Bible or any religion but you must remember that this does not equal an indictment of God.

The depth of understanding and self revelation which I received from a singular dream picture represented a means of imparting a quantum of knowledge in an instant which would have taken perhaps years to decipher with any rational approach. This imparting of an idea or concept with one image is beyond rational thought. Rational thought is crippled by preconceptions and factual assumptions. Insight is the acquisition of pure knowledge in an instant, it is turning the light on in a dark room.

WHY NOT AN ATHEIST

I have been a practicing attorney for twenty years now. I have spent many years in the court room pouring over evidence, dissecting and uncovering the truth. There is no other forum where the lies which people tell can be subject to such intense scrutiny and cross examination. There is no skill which is quite as dramatic to watch as a seasoned trial lawyer taking apart a witness under cross examination. It is like finding a very small loose thread, just barely visible and pulling at it, tugging at it until that small almost invisible thread, that lie, causes the whole intricate structure of the fabric to unravel before your eyes. Although the courtroom is the place where people lie most often, they sometimes are not aware of their own delusions from which the lies grow. Their self interest changes the lens with which they view past events to such a degree in some cases that there is no similarity between the event and the later recollection of the event.

A thorough examination of the truth is not possible without protagonists who are firmly entrenched in their own sides "righteousness". The logical protagonist to the idea of a god or any spiritual leader in this case would be the atheist. He has taken the extreme position that there is no God or Gods at all. Of course interestingly enough there are "hard" atheists and "soft" atheists. The former believing that there is no God and the later having no belief in God. We will use the "hard" atheists as our guide as we want a truly representative example of why we should choose atheism. We want the best case possible that can be made that there is no God because in the end we are seeking the truth no matter what it might be. We want to know what atheism can do for us as individuals that we cannot do for ourselves.

Although I professed to be an atheist in my youth, I never really had any detailed knowledge of what they actually believed. I only knew what they didn't believe in any power greater★ than themselves called God. At that youthful window in my life that was sufficient.

After a diligent search of the atheist sites on the internet I was surprised to discover that they have very little to say about what they do believe, only that they do not believe in God. They believe that a belief in God has created nothing good in the world and the sooner that silly notion is buried deep in the earth, from where it can never rise again, the better off we will all be.

We must attempt to first define and circumscribe the argument which the atheist will make as it relates to their lack of belief in an omniscient, omnipresent, supreme entity. A search of the internet reveals certain basic beliefs held by at least one faction of atheists. The following is a direct quote from one such website.

"First, let me lay my cards on the table: I am an atheist—a ★hard★ atheist. I find the Christian/Jewish/Muslim concept of God to be inherently illogical and I consider the "Holy

Books" of these religions to be a naive collection of myths cobbled together from preexisting ideas and texts."

"However, I also maintain, as do most atheists, that my position is a rational one based on evidence or the lack of it. Thus my beliefs are hostage to the data and, at least in principle, there is the possibility that they will be falsified by some new evidence."

It is critical to analyze with an objective eye the evidence and position which the atheist will take in disabusing us of a belief in God. We can identify the major points in this atheist's argument as follows:

1. He considers the Christian/Jewish/Muslim concept of God to be inherently illogical
2. He considers the "Holy Books" of these religions to be a naïve collection of myths cobbled together from preexisting ideas and texts
3. He maintains that his position is a rational one based on evidence or lack of it.
4. His beliefs are hostage to the data and in principle there is a possibility that they will be falsified by some new evidence.

IS THE CONCEPT OF GOD
INHERENTLY ILLOGICAL

L ogic is defined as follows: the science that investigates the principles governing correct or reliable inference. 2. a particular method of reasoning or argumentation: We were unable to follow his logic. 3. the system or principles of reasoning applicable to any branch of knowledge or study.

So what this particular atheist is saying for the believers in atheism is that the "concept" of God is inherently not reasonable when subjected to the methodology of "logical reasoning" as invented by man. It is clear that he has in fact not denied that there is a God but only that the existing concepts which have been proffered by certain religions is illogical according to certain manmade rules of logical examination. Of course the obvious presumption which is being used as a foundation for all his other arguments is that "logic" is the supreme rule of the universe subject to no higher order of understanding the truth. The more perplexing part of the argument, if examined logically, is that if God cannot be "comprehended" by man through his logical machinations then he surely cannot exist. The implication of that argument is that if anything cannot be comprehended by man's reasoning then it clearly does not exist. That does not sound like a persuasive argument to me. There are an infinite number of things which logic and science cannot explain.

My most current example is a client I had who suffered a trauma to his foot. He was shot by an air rifle at close range and over time he developed a "desmoid tumor" in the location where he was shot. In my deposition of the orthopedic surgeon and the Pediatric Oncologist they both stated that the origin of a tumor was difficult to ascertain or determine to an absolute certainty. Although this tumor arose in exactly the same area where the boy was shot the highly educated professionals could not testify with absolute certainty as to how it had arisen although they did know that desmoid tumors arise as a result of trauma. They also know that they sometimes just appear with no apparent causation. They had subjected the tumor to every known diagnostic methodology developed through man's reasoning abilities and with all that arsenal of logic and scientific lore they were unable to positively say with an absolute certainty how the tumor had arisen. It was clear, however, that they knew the tumor had originated as a result of the trauma of the shot to the foot but they were held hostage by the logic which suggested it could have been some other causation. They had no answer which could not be attacked by reason and because of that they would not give any definitive answer.

The probabilities suggested the shot to the foot but the physicians hesitated to state it as a certainty. The question then has to be to this "hard atheist" who has based his opening and closing arguments on the failure of the existence of God to yield to "man's reason", If two physicians cannot with certainty determine the genesis of a desmoid tumor, something which can be seen, touched and examined with cutting edge technology, then how can God be dismissed so casually because he or it cannot be explained by man's reason. It is clear that man's reason is limited by man's concept and knowledge of the known world. The only possible screening criteria which he could utilize to analyze the rational from the irrational would be based on his existing knowledge of his corner of the rational universe.

One more short story from my childhood would, I believe, be important to define what we can know and what we cannot know of this world. I was perhaps ten years old and my family consisting of my three brothers and mother and father were sitting around the dinner table having our family dinner. We were living in Altus, Oklahoma at the time, but we had only been there for less than a year which was about average for us. The phone rang and my father answered it. As soon as the phone rang, before it was even picked up I knew what the call was about. I knew exactly what critical piece of news was about to be delivered to my father. I knew that someone was calling to tell him that his mother, my grandmother had died. That was all I knew but I knew it with a certainty on which I would have bet my life. It was a piece of information which just appeared in my consciousness and ever since that day I have often wondered how it got there. There was no conversation about her. I had only met her once and I don't recall that she was even sick. My father as far as I could remember never talked to her and she lived in New Mexico. She was not an important person in my life, however, I often think that it was her spirit which sought me out and perhaps passed through me leaving the knowledge of her death behind.

I don't believe that you could find anyone who has directly experienced God who could consider God capable of being understood under any methodology created by man especially a logical one. I know that in my own personal experience of God there was nothing which I could explain rationally or logically. It is perhaps this disdain in our society for all things illogical, especially among those who consider themselves intellectuals to dismiss any concept which has not been blessed by the sacred trinity of, reason, logic and rationalism. It was certainly one of the reasons I did not and still do not advertise my new found enthusiasm for an inherently irrational concept which I know will draw only derision from a culture which worships all things rational and mocks all things which do not bow at the altar of reason.

It is easy to see why the atheist and the believer have a difficult time understanding the other's position. The atheist only sees things through his rational lens and the believer, (at least the ones who have had a direct experience of God) know beyond a shadow of a doubt what they experienced and what it has meant to their lives. They speak different languages and they are both "true believers" in their own Gods.

In summary of point one it is clear that the "religious concepts of God" have been found illogical by the atheists but they have made the basic error of equating God with man's concepts of God. They have not only applied the wrong methodology to the discovery of the existence of God but they have applied it to the description of the object and not the object itself.

IS IT RELEVANT TO THE EXISTENCE OF GOD THAT THE "HOLY BOOKS" OF THESE RELIGIONS MAYBE A NAIVE COLLECTION OF MYTHS?

> Rationalism, which is the feeling that everything is subject to and completely explicable by Reason, consequently rejects everything not visible and calculable.
>
> Francis Parker Yockey

I do not believe that God could ever be captured in any holy books or any books at all. I do believe that there are certain useful stories, lessons and examples which are helpful in seeking God. Whether those stories are myths, reality or a mix of both is irrelevant to the determination of the existence of God. A nexus of power which is omnipresent, omnipotent and infinite, all knowing and the creative center of all that we see and do not see cannot be defined by man nor contained in the pages of any book.

The logical or illogical content of these books is secondary to their ability to make us meditate and consider the existence of an organizing creative force which governs all that is known and unknown. It is the power of these books to take us in the direction of God that is their greatness, their holiness. They plant a seed which allows us to understand certain experiences which happen to us which are beyond the reach of reason or rationalism to explain. If God is all things then he is both rational and irrational and then some.

The search for God, like the search for anything else whether the nucleus of an atom or the origin of dark matter in the Universe must be conducted without the interference of any preconceived ideas or methodologies which only hinder and blind us to possibilities which we deem irrational. A rational explanation is one based on certain factual presumptions which may or may not be objectively true but when strung together lead to the rational conclusion desired.

The Universe existed before rationalism and despite our apparent dependence on it to save us from ourselves it is an imperfect system. Let us consider the following examples of the limitations of rationalism. Once again a search of "rationalism" on the internet yields some interesting information concerning its limitations.

"It is believed by some philosophers (notably A.C. Grayling) that a good rationale must be independent of emotions, personal feelings or any kind of instincts. Any process of evaluation or analysis, that may be called rational, is expected to be highly objective, logical and "mechanical". "If these minimum requirements are not satisfied i.e. if a person has been, even slightly, influenced by personal emotions, feelings, instincts or culturally specific, moral codes and norms, then the analysis may be termed irrational, due to the injection of subjective bias."

"It is evident from modern cognitive science and neuroscience, studying the role of emotion in mental function (including topics ranging from flashes of scientific insight to making future plans), that no human has ever satisfied this criterion, except perhaps a person with no affective feelings, for example an individual with a massively damaged amygdala or severe psychopathy. Thus, such an idealized form of rationality is best exemplified by computers, and not people. However, scholars may productively appeal to the idealization as a point of reference. In furtherance of this line of thought I came across this passage"

"In light of this rational finding concerning the limitations of "rationalism" it appears that it is not possible for a human being to exercise a pure form of rationality. Our human rationalism will always be colored by our emotions and experiences."

"The relationship between rationality and political power was studied by Flyvberg (1998). He found that in real-life decision making rationality is context-dependent and the context of rationality is power. Thus power profoundly influences rationality, and what decision makers think of and present as rationality is often a rationalization of power positions, according to Flyvbjerg. In a paraphrase of Blaise Pascal, Flyvbjerg concludes that "power has a rationality that rationality does not know."

The god of Rationality, at least appears to be less than all powerful as its power is limited by human emotions, experiences and feelings (the context). Interestingly enough this collection of "context" may be described as a naïve collection of myths cobbled together from preexisting ideas, emotions, feelings and texts.

IS IT REASONABLE THAT THE ATHEIST MAINTAINS HIS POSITION IS A RATIONAL ONE BASED ON EVIDENCE OR LACK OF IT?

—————❧—————

In light of our discussion on the limitations of Rational thought we could probably all agree that the Atheist's arguments are circumscribed by his" context" much as are the non-atheist's reasons for believing in God. This argument must then be given the "weight" which it deserves in relation to its evidentiary significance in proving that God does not exist. If it is true that the "context" defines the result then there is very little "weight", from an objective perspective, that can be given to a rational argument for or against the existence of God.

God is too big to be defined. Any definition or effort to circumscribe God is doomed from the start as being too small, too confining, too restrictive to be corralled by words or concepts built on words. How would you describe the essence of an apple to someone who had never seen an apple. Even in this simple example words do not impart the reality of the apple. You must touch it, smell it and taste it before you really understand what an apple is. Words or concepts or books about the apple would always fall far short of the essence of the apple. How much truer is this of God yet those who attack the concept of God attack the concepts, words, books and theisms which attempt to describe God. They are not attempting to be God; they are attempting to describe God.

If we were to take the apple analogy further this is what it would look like. A long time ago there were a few individuals on this planet who had direct contact with an apple. They had encountered one, held it, tasted it and even consumed it. In this hypothetical apples are quite rare and have been directly experienced by an unknown number of people but written about by many. Some of those writers had a personal experience with the apple and others had not but wrote about it anyway. The skeptics who did not believe in apples asked probing questions about it. They wanted to know from whence it had come, how it could be many different colors and shapes, how it could be one color on the inside and another on the outside. When told that the apple came from a tree that came from a seed they wanted to know where the seed came from. The seed could not have just mysteriously appeared, the skeptics would say. Only someone with limited intelligence would swallow such a ridiculous argument especially when the believers proclaimed the apple to be a magic fruit which could impart wonderful benefits to your body if consumed regularly.

I would probably be on the side of the skeptics on this one. The story has too many loose ends which can't be explained. How big is this seed? How big is the tree and how many apples come from the tree that came from only one small seed. I don't think so. I am certainly not that gullible. Now perhaps if I stumbled upon an apple tree and recognized it from my readings about it I might change my mind about the existence of apples. There are just some things which you just have to see to believe. Besides I was not born yesterday and I didn't just get off the boat.

Finally the atheist's parting point leaves a clear exit strategy for him when and if he is presented any evidence which would change his mind. This is certainly a rational tactic although it appears to be more "posturing" to give the appearance of open and free thinking. Rationalism as in any "ism" limits the concept of "open and free" thinking to only concepts which that particular "ism" has codified. The sacred trinity of rationalism, reason and scientific inquiry will never be threatened by the atheist's most determined efforts at "open and free" thinking.

WHY ARE HIS BELIEFS HOSTAGE TO THE DATA AND IS THERE IS A POSSIBILITY THEY COULD BE FALSIFIED BY NEW DATA?

—— ❧ ——

> With most people disbelief in a thing is founded
> on a blind belief in some other thing.
>
> Georg C Lichtenberg (1742-1799)
> German scientist, satirist and anglophile.

This truly sounds like "legal speak" when an attorney is leaving a loop hole just in case it turns out he was wrong in his original conclusion. This is probably a smart move if there is indeed a supreme intelligence which is aware of our opinion of its existence and is capable of meting out justice based on that.

In reality all beliefs are hostage to the data from which they took birth. Whether the belief was that the world was flat, that there was no water on Mars, or that we are not causing global warming they are all hostage to the "context" from which they were birthed. It all comes down to the "context" of the search defining the parameters of the discovery or belief. You cannot find a sunken treasure in the

Pacific Ocean using a treasure map of the Atlantic Ocean. You cannot rationally critique religions established by man to formalize their worship of a God and call it proof that a God does not exist.

Is it possible that this is the best argument that the Atheist can offer or even the most prevalent belief of atheists? Clearly if given thoughtful consideration it is not a particularly convincing argument. I do not believe that it is persuasive. Perhaps God would accept a compromise and agree that he is not the God of the rationalists but only of all the other weak minded souls who have only experienced the fundamental transformation which he has brought into their lives.

Is direct proof, experiential proof superior to rational proof? If you were to ask any person who has had an actual real life experience of a power greater than themselves acting in their lives they would answer with a solid yes. The experience of God in your life is something that is never forgotten and always desired. It is uplifting, nurturing, calming and always life altering. It is inaccessible by way of reason. Perhaps for those who rely solely on their reason to navigate through the mystery of life they are doomed to forever be ignorant of God even though he is standing right in front of them on the street corner. Those persons who are able to use their reasoning powers judiciously and access their intuitive and instinctive powers when appropriate are much more likely to encounter God in their life.

The Atheist is tenacious in his belief that if the believer was just as smart and intellectually advanced as he was there wouldn't be all this nonsense about a fairy living in the sky that can make everything bad into a picnic in the park. The intellectual arrogance displayed by non believers act as blinders to any free or creative thinking related to God. It can also be argued that most theist sects do exactly the same thing. It is really interesting to note how similar the aims of the atheist and the believers are when examined.

The atheist perspective also includes a desire to replace organized deist religions with their philosophy. They believe that they are in fact the "good news" and living as an atheist would solve all the world's problems. An excerpt from another atheist website reveals a "Christian like approach" to saving the world through atheism.

"Your petitioners are atheists, and they define their lifestyle as follows. An atheist loves himself and his fellow man instead of a god. An atheist accepts that heaven is something for which we should work now—here on earth—for all men together to enjoy. An atheist accepts that he can get no help through prayer, but that he must find in himself the inner conviction and strength to meet life, to grapple with it, to subdue it and to enjoy it. An atheist accepts that only in a knowledge of himself and a knowledge of his fellow man can he find the understanding that will help lead to a life of fulfillment."

"No philosophy, no religion, has ever brought
so glad a message to the world as this good news
of Atheism."

—*Annie Wood Besant*

"What exactly does an atheist believe?" Now for the first time we have something to explore as it relates to what it is that motivates people who dismiss the reality of God. What is it that they want and do they have any rules for behavior in society which is any different from any of the major religious faiths.

"An atheist loves himself and his fellow man instead of a god." I am not sure what the significance of this statement is other than it implies that a theist cannot love himself and his fellow man if he loves God. The statement alone suggests a naïve and uninformed concept of what the believer actually believes and how he conducts himself in his daily life. Once again when I refer to believers I am focusing on those who did not deny their God when faced with retribution for their beliefs. They held fast in the face of torture and death. This was a small group of believers historically and it is a small group of believers now. It would be naïve on my part to think that everyone that professed to being a good Christian, Jew, Muslim, Hindu, Buddhist or Taoist was in fact living out their faith especially in the face of real life adversity. I understand the atheist disenchantment with theists who wage wars in the name of God, burn non-believers at the stake, condemn believers of other faiths to burn in Hell, and blow themselves up in crowded public places in the name of Allah.

I have known many self professed religious people who fail to grasp the most basic concepts of compassion, love, faith, belief and righteousness. These are the religionists who create atheists and taint the true nature of "morality" with their religious posturing usually to gain some personal advantage. I knew a man who had donated tens of thousands of dollars to his favorite church where he was a Deacon. He was admired by the church leaders and the congregation as a man of God. In reality he was a dishonest con man who spent large sums of money on mistresses in Asia while forcing his wife to survive on an allowance which compelled her to collect aluminum cans from trash bins to pay for her necessities of life. There are millions of similar stories worldwide.

These are the people who mock God and create disillusionment about any higher power who would allow such a practice to persist. Stories of believers who have done horrible and ugly things abound. Stories of religious leaders who have perpetrated evil acts against their flock and misled them with slick lies and promises of salvation can be found in every religion and sect. The atheist or other non believer rationally comprehends the evil in these acts and catalogues another example of why he should not believe in a God who would allow such wrongs to exist in his name.

Despite this, however, the fundamental principal illustrated most clearly in the story of Adam and Eve in the Garden of Eden when they were told they could eat of any tree in the garden except one tree was free will. God gave man free will. It can be postulated that he gave it to him so that man would come to him freely without coercion. It is only in this act of free will that God can be assured that mans choice to believe is just that a "freely chosen path". We cannot therefore nor can God's detractors blame man's "unrighteous behavior" on God. Man must take the responsibility for his acts, for his thoughts, for his deeds and misdeeds before he can mold himself into the image of God.

An impartial examination of our thoughts and acts and their transformation into our problems or solutions reveals that we control our own destinies including the extent of God's participation.

The atheists have made it clear that they have no place for a supreme being (other than man) in shaping their destiny. They believe that they can get no help from prayer but it is puzzling how they arrived at that conclusion. Did they try praying and they did not get what they wanted and therefore came to the conclusion? Did they pray for no wars, more rain, more money, a new car, a new job, or merely a stop to all the injustice in the world? Do they believe that prayers must be answered in direct accordance with the request, without any deviation? I have read that some atheists come to their "belief" by noting the sad state of the world and asking why any benevolent God would ever let such atrocities happen. They are unable to come to a reasonable conclusion to their questions and as such assume the absence of any such power.

If we follow their dicta that the answer is in man alone and that man must have "the conviction and strength to meet life, grapple with it and subdue it and to enjoy it." Let's assume for the sake of argument that the atheists are right and there is no God. We then have to look at the world as it is today and instead of blaming an unseen, nonexistent God we must blame man. The same man whom the atheists put their supreme faith in to solve all of our problems is in fact the cause of all of our problems. It is man who commits the atrocities, kills the planet, lays waste to most of what he touches and still trumpets his intelligence and problem solving abilities. I say it is very fortunate for the atheists that there are people who believe in God because without that God the atheist would have to take responsibility for the mess we find ourselves in, according to the statement of their own convictions.

If the atheist is right that only a knowledge of himself and his fellow man will lead to a life of fulfillment then why are we where we are now? What is this knowledge of himself that the atheist talks about? It has to be knowledge within the rational sphere but we have volumes and volumes of scientific knowledge regarding mankind. We have more detailed and extensive knowledge about how man works both physically and psychologically then at any other time in the history of the world. During the centuries within which this information has been amassed has the world become a better place? Do we even have to answer that question?

Furthermore if this isn't the knowledge of self and others which we need to increase what knowledge is it? It can't be a spiritual knowledge because that does not exist. If the atheist "way" is in fact all we have we are in big trouble. The atheist manifesto is of the material world. All things arise and perish on the material plane. There is nothing else out there, just you, me and the TV. The atheist believes that he must have "the conviction and inner strength to meet life, grapple with it and subdue it to enjoy it".

We have to ask then where does this inner strength and conviction come from? What exactly is this inner strength and conviction? Assuming the conviction creates the inner strength (much as the theists' belief in God can give him inner strength and conviction). What could this wonderful knowledge be that creates such a tremendous conviction and strength? Of course for theists it is a belief in something greater than man that actually rules the universe. It not only rules the universe but it can be accessed by man and if its rules are understood sufficiently by man it can be a powerful ally to all man's efforts in his life. The atheist also believes that he must overcome life and subdue it in order to enjoy it. I will assume that this means he must win as much as possible in his life and gather as many material trophies during his lifetime so that he can enjoy life.

This is the enjoyment of the material plane which can be described as a bounty of excess which guarantees comfort and security for their time on this planet. This leads me to believe that the atheist is to be found among those who do not suffer want or deprivation more often than those who suffer deprivation. Perhaps money is the atheist's God, as money can certainly buy enjoyment and enough money can subdue life and overcome life's hardships. If the atheists were to nominate a God I believe that money might be a suitable candidate. The atheist party line is that the more intelligent person, usually those more well off than the uneducated, are more likely to be atheists. I suppose if you never had a crisis in your life which you didn't lack sufficient money to alleviate then why would you need a God, you are God. It is conceivable that the knowledge that the atheist has is the balance in his bank account and the value of his stock portfolio. I cannot think of any other possibility which would satisfy the criteria of the atheist to the degree money would.

We know that money is power and that with power comes strength and conviction in our own righteousness. We also know that money is the ruler of the material plane and we all remember the succinct verse that states it so clearly in the "golden rule". He who has the gold rules. Our society of rampant robotic consumerism worships the dollar and the power with which it is imbued.

Man has structured his world to survive and he has accomplished this to a degree that no other mammal has been able to. He has risen to the top of the mammalian food chain and in the process has subdued or eliminated his closest rivals for the necessities of life. He has invented governments, religions, philosophies, cities, electricity, plastic bags, throw away diapers and an endless array of other consumer goods which support his life on this planet. He has bred freely and multiplied his numbers geometrically. The species now covers the planet finding no climate too challenging for his ingenuity. He has travelled into space and to the bottom of the oceans. He has reason to boast. He has conquered all that has set itself in front of him and he has done it without help. He appears to be the reigning deity of the material plane.

It is not until we examine man more closely that we wonder where it is this power over nature has taken us. Anyone taking a breath these days knows the answer to that one. The answer is not pretty and it is not comforting. It does not allow us to rest peacefully in our beds at night and it does not allow us the luxury of enjoying life without liberal doses of medicine, alcohol or drugs to jump start our elusive moments when we enjoy life. It has not given us the power to control our own addictions. The majority of us have an insatiable, unquenchable, and inexhaustible appetite for more of everything. The problem with that appetite is that on the material plane everything is finite. There is a limited number of everything which you can see and with ever increasing numbers of our species there arises and ever increasing and aggressively ugly competition for those always decreasing luxuries and necessities of which the material plane is composed. The contrast to that is the spiritual plane which is infinite and its treasures of peace, compassion, love and forgiveness are unlimited. The more you have the more there is to have. There is no need to compete. There is no need to fight or go to war for the things of the spiritual world. You only need to slow down and look inside for that is where they are hiding. After all everything arises from the inside and proceeds to the outside. The apple seed contains the tree, the blossoms, the bark, the leaves, the colors, the smell, the taste and of course the apples.

What a wonderful thing a seed is. We all come from seeds. That is where we started. A seed so small it cannot even be seen with the naked eye. That seed contained everything which is you in a mysterious world within its invisible soul. I believe that it is possible to reach a spiritual enlightenment simply my meditating every day of your life on this simple concept. It all comes from the seed the source of everything which is called apple. If life itself is not a miracle then there are no miracles. Our problem is that is it so close to us we cannot appreciate the wonder of our own existence, the brilliance of our design and the infinite depth and breadth of our spirit which links us all as one. We only see the differences because they are children of the material plane and the material plane forgets from whence it came.

Madalyn Murry Ohair, the most well known atheist in our time, would not be a poster child for atheism. Her fulfilled life would have to be defined as being the success of her attempts to stop prayer in schools. She did what she set out to do and as a result has left a lasting legacy. As to her finding fulfillment in her personal life, the accounts of her life fall short of the mark. She was often described as a task master to those under her. She was someone who had no consideration for her followers and "often cursed them, wrote terrible things about them and fired them after they had worked for a pittance and made sacrifices for her" She was disliked even hated by many in the atheist community and it was said that she did more harm than good for their cause.

Her life ended tragically in her brutal murder and dismemberment by an employee who hatched a plot to extort and murder her, her son and her granddaughter. There were initially allegations of her stealing money from the American Atheists organization as some five hundred thousand dollars in gold coins went missing when she did. It is an interesting fact to note that the article stated that her followers were seduced by her brilliance.

If this is a life of fulfillment count me out. I wonder if in those last minutes of life she considered reaching out to a God who could save her or comfort her. Did she pray, if I was her I would have. If she came face to face with evil then I hope she found faith in something bigger than herself. The God that I know would have comforted her if she had merely turned and asked for that comfort. I really don't think she would have found any comfort in recalling the balance in her bank account. I also do not think that her brilliance offered her any comfort.

THE SECOND DREAM,
IS GOD FOLLOWING ME

The second dream in the series of religious dreams which I had concerned an invisible entity whose footsteps could be seen following me wherever I went. My life leading up to this dream was in the early stages of my return to religion as marked by the dream of the drowning cathedral. I had been incessantly reading books on God and religion searching for clues as to how, when and where I could make contact with God if he existed. I was still intrigued by the idea of God following me around my entire life knocking on my door waiting for me to answer. Of course following is really the wrong word because the reality of God is he is there, everywhere all the time and it only takes our attention on him to become aware of his presence.

This resurgence of religiosity caused me to consider all the times in my life when I actually had a feeling of "knowing" exactly what I should do in terms of decisions. Along with the confidence of what to do I also had a lack of fear of the outcome of those actions a certainty of their "rightness". Although I did not, at the time, equate this assurance with a God who was protecting and guiding me I knew instinctively what was the right and wrong move to make. Looking back on those days in perspective of my dream I realized, just as I had foreknowledge of my grandmother's death, that God had always been by my side. That confidence and certainty that I had came from him. It was his gift to me and to all of us if we just open our minds and hearts and listen. But it is so difficult to listen, really listen and wait and then listen some more and wait some more. The combination of listening and waiting throws many people off the trail of God; it takes patience and faith in the outcome. It takes time.

I was heavily into Zen Buddhism, Taoism, Sufism and Shamanism and was influenced by the action without thought modality which was stressed. It was the philosophy most succinctly expressed by the story of the old man who was hiking by the raging mountain stream which cascaded down the steep mountain. The old man suddenly jumped into the swift moving waters and disappeared from sight. Minutes later he could be seen popping out of the torrent and back on the shore, no worse for the wear. To me that exemplified an attitude of trust in the "Way" or the flow of life. Plunging headfirst into the raging torrent of life and knowing, no not even knowing, but just being without fear, that is living, that is the rush God, whoever he, she or it may be, delivers.

This is very similar to the trust I have now developed in God who I experience as being at my side at all times. He is watching over me, guiding me, and leading me to higher experiences and a broader view of the possibilities of my life then I could possibly have had using my own limited facilities. I do not even pretend anymore that there is no higher power than myself or humankind. At this point in my life I find that belief to be a naïve and foolish idea whose life expectancy should be limited to the first "real crisis" you experience in your life. In this dream I knew that it was merely a reminder to me that I had always been watched over despite where my beliefs might have been. That abiding sense I had of invincibility and confidence in my actions arose from my belief in a higher power that offered protection to all of us without consciously manifesting the belief as a belief in God.

In the dream I was once again looking down but this time on a valley. I saw myself driving a vehicle that reminded me of a golf cart but wasn't one. I was taking a meandering route and I noticed that behind the card, wherever I went footsteps appeared. I could see them being made but there was no person associated with the tracks just the appearance of one foot after another as my cart moved forward.

It was clear to me that this dream related to the knocking on my door idea because these footprints left by some invisible being were God's footprints. I knew from this dream that my entire life God had been right there with me guiding me, protecting me, advising me and gently pushing me in the direction he wanted me to go. My life has not been a linear progression from A to Z but instead has taken the circuitous path of a bird in flight. I know now after the perspective of a man of advanced age and a lifetime of experience that God was always there. This thought alone is enough to change a person's life. It was certainly enough to transform the way I approached mine. I was removed from the center of my universe and surrendered to the "way of life" the creative force called God that had safely brought me through a myriad of dangerous and sometimes life threatening challenges. The blinders had been taken off and I could now see that I was not the only one making things happen in my life. I had help.

I did not have to rationally analyze the dream because I "knew" what it meant and that its message was dead on. It was an "ah ha" moment, a moment of spiritual advancement and human growth. I basked in the idea that God actually watched over me and protected me. I still remember the prayer that I used to say back then night after night because it helped to quell the storm of anxiety and doubt which disturbed my sleep every night. "I cry out to you O Lord because I know you will answer me. Give me your ear so that you might hear my prayer. Show me the wonder of your infinite and unconditional love, for you are the one who saved those who sought refuge in you from their enemies. Keep me as the apple of your eye. Hide me in the shadow of your wings from the wicked and evil who assail me and my mortal enemies who seek to destroy me".

God sent this prayer to me in one of the many books which I read at that time and it was exactly what I needed. During that time he sent me many prayers and thoughts that carried me through these difficult times. Each one was exactly on point and delivered at precisely the time when I most needed it. He was talking to me. He was guiding me out of the heart of darkness through the valley of desolation into the light. Each thought, each prayer which he gave me was a small miracle which he worked in my life. It wasn't winning the lottery. It was better, much better.

It was during this time that I began to learn the transformative power of prayer. Prayer is the perfect action as it transforms the person who prays. My first thought was this was just silly but I was willing to try. I believe that it was the "trying" that matters not the nature of the act. It could be prayer or any other turning to God. God will respond and it is a beautiful thing especially if it is all new to you and so unexpected. I have come to believe that God is trying to communicate with us continually, not only through dreams but also books, media, other persons and any other medium with which he might be able to catch our attention for just one minute. He is the master of communication if we only take the time to listen, to feel, to experience outside of the walls of our rational existence with all its dead ends and wrong turns.

I will have to tell a short story about God's desire for me to write this book. I have in years past written two books. One was self published and the other is in my desk drawer after having been exhaustively shopped around without any takers. I always thought that after I retired, still some five years in the future I would once again pursue writing. God did not have the same time frame in mind as I did. I will mention that when I was led to start writing I was working full time as an attorney in my own firm which was very busy.

I had very little time to do anything but run my office. I was then as I still am now voraciously consuming books related to God.

It was my noon break from the office and I had stopped at the local Seven Eleven to grab some water. As I was pulling into the parking lot of the store an old lady was crossing the street. I had seen her before at least once and at first glance she appeared to be homeless. I would gauge her age to be maybe sixty to seventy with an oriental look about her. She was short; perhaps five foot two and weighed maybe a hundred pounds. When I had seen her before she was at the bank parking lot, this first time she was also facing me and making strange gestures with her arms and hands. I was in a hurry and had no time for a homeless woman who was apparently mad.

As it is with homeless people we do not want to stare especially if they appear mentally unstable. That was the impression which I was left with the first time I saw her. The second time was the parking lot incident which I am describing. As I was turning into the lot she crossed the street directly in front of me. There were no crosswalks and no lights. As she walked in front of me I looked at her more closely. I noticed to my surprise that she had a knit hat on which looked clean and new. Her clothing which hung in layers also appeared clean, well fitted and simple. My impression of being homeless immediately changed to one of perhaps a widow who lived on a limited income but considered the cleanliness of her person as a necessity. When she crossed to the other side she retrieved a hand cart, the type you see made of wire with wheels and a pull handle to carry items in, from the bushes. The contents were nondescript. She was standing there over her cart when I entered the store. I had parked in the lot with my car facing the other side of the street where she had gone.

I came out of the store and sat in my car resting a few minutes before returning to the office and drank my water. Looking out the front window of my car I noticed the woman immediately in the center of my vision facing me. She was framed by a wooden sign whose support posts rose vertically while the bottom of the actual sign cut across horizontally at the height of some two feet above the woman's head. The affect was that she was framed directly in my line of vision by the rectangle which was formed by the supports and the bottom of the sign. It was like watching a flat screen television from my sofa. She was standing on the sidewalk on the opposite side of the street facing me. Her shoulders were squared and her feet spread at about shoulder width. He hands were at waist height in front of her bent at the elbows in an almost ninety degree angle to her upper arms.

She started making what appeared to be random movements with her hands and arms while she directly faced my vehicle. There were cars passing on the roadway between us but I cannot recall that they interfered at all with the message which she was delivering to me. I sensed that she was there for me and I needed to pay attention so I did very careful attention.

She faced me and the shawl that covered her shoulders also covered her entire right hand. Her left hand was visible. The most notable motion was the uncontrollable jerking motion of her right arm and hand. Like a person with palsy who could not control the movement of a limb. The right hand jerked vigorously up and down in frantic short strokes. It was like she was pounding something but it was an uncontrolled action which she would watch with what appeared to be some detachment and then she would calmly take her left hand and hold onto her right hand, which was covered by the shawl, until the frantic up and down motion stopped. This holding and releasing her right hand by her left hand continued for five minutes. I sat and watched trying to understand what was happening.

After maybe ten repetitions of this cycle the right hand stopped moving in its' sporadic up and down motion. The hand itself appeared from beneath the shawl and she moved the shawl farther up her forearms to free both her hands. As she faced me she then started moving both her hands as if she were playing a piano. The hands moved rhythmically back and forth across the keyboard in short but precise motion. The imaginary keyboard was positioned at waist height in front of her. I watched her while she methodically and repeatedly moved her fingers across the keyboard. All of her motions were controlled; there were no more jerky movements of her right hand. She had assumed control of both of her hands now which gracefully worked the keyboard. As if recall it now I can't remember how long I watched or where she was when I finally left. I thought about this throughout the afternoon and that night I found a quiet spot so that I could concentrate on what I had seen and then I knew.

She was typing. She was telling me to start writing, now. It was time now to start, not five years from now but right now. The out of control hidden right hand symbolized the worldly distractions and addictive behaviors which needed to be controlled in order to write. She told me what I needed to do and how I needed to do it. I started writing that night and it brought me a sense of peace. I wrote every night until I finished this book. Who was it that sent that woman to me to communicate this message? Could it have been God using her to be his messenger? I think it was.

WHY DO WE BELIEVE

The question now is why humans believe anything. We are all aware that much of the knowledge we have is in the form of a belief. The definition of belief is as follows.

1. An acceptance that a statement is true or that something exists.
2. Something one accepts as true or real; a firmly held opinion or conviction

So how is it that we reach a point that we accept some statement as true or that something exists? How do we get to the point where we believe that something is true or real? The obvious way is through our experience. As an example we should pick something in which we all believe. We all believe that the Sun will rise in the East and set in the West each and every day of our lives. Now we believe this to be true because we have experienced it. We have all experienced it every day of our lives. It is an event which can be predicted, measured, seen, felt, and which causes us to feel and act in certain ways. It is an event which happens on the material plane and is easily examined.

Some of us are morning people who like to get up early, sometimes before the Sun rises. The air is brisk and fresh and the day is just combing the night out of its hair and preparing for the long day ahead. Everything is new and there is hope and endless prospects. There are also those who prefer the evening. The day is stretching its sore joints and muscles from a long day of activity. The night is arriving in its own time, in no hurry as it knows it will soon reign supreme. It will cast its dark shadow over all things and suddenly the world is full of unknown forms, noises and forbidden secrets. But regardless of which you are you believe in the cycles of the Sun because you have directly experienced them. You do not need a scientific journal to make you a believer you just need to open your eyes and pay attention. The Sun phenomenon can be experienced by our senses and processed by our minds, rationally processed. These traits make belief easy. We will see later however discover that even these obvious observations of material reality might not be what we think they are.

A more difficult example would be love. There are many people who believe in love because they have had a direct experience of love. There are also many people who do not believe because they have never been in love. There are those who do not believe in love but they have read about love or heard others describe love and they have to decide whether or not they believe in love because they have never felt the power of love to make each day another day in heaven basking in pure joy or the agony and anguish of love tearing at the walls of their heart from the inside out. They have never surrendered themselves to another or been willing to die for another. Despite that some of these people will profess a belief in love, perhaps it is the "cool" thing to do and besides most people do not want to confess that they have never been in love. It sounds so wonderful and all the movies make it look so delicious. If only they could find the right person they could be in love. There are also those that believe that the physical act of making love is the same as love. This is most certainly a large group in our culture. Even though love is such an important concept in our culture we cannot all agree on what it is or what it feels like to be in love.

Those who have borderline experiences of love are not however the ones who would sacrifice their lives for their belief in love because despite their protestations of love they have never really experienced it, borne the pain and joy of it. Those believers who were mentioned early in this book who gave their lives for their belief in God did so because they had the direct experience of God. They knew to an absolute certainty and with complete faith what their sacrificed their self for. The God they knew personally was the God they loved personally. It was a love like that of a parent who loves his child beyond anything else and would be willing to die for that child without a moment's hesitation. Those people who have never loved someone or something else cannot possibly understand this self sacrifice. In fact I would speculate that they would say it was ridiculous, a fairy tale and a silly myth which had no basis in reality. They would probably also attempt to rationalize why it is impossible for love to exist or if it did exist to cause someone to give their life for someone else. I think we can comfortably say that love is a personal experience which although having some common characteristics is different for all of us.

Those people who have experienced love cannot be persuaded that it does not exist. They can however be deeply saddened by someone who attempts to convince them that it does not exist. Their sadness is due to the great loss they know the non-believer in love has suffered. Their hearts go out to that person and with their whole hearts they wish that they might find love. The question then becomes whether someone has to believe in something before they can actually experience that something to the degree that they develop a working belief in it. Is it possible for the person who does not believe in love to ever actually be in love?

If we return to the example of belief in the Sun then the answer to the question of whether or not you have to believe in the Sun setting in the West and rising in the East before you can experience it is a resounding no. The answer is no because you can see for yourself and test for yourself the objective material reality of the Sun's movements because it exists in the material plane. Love, however, is a different beast which lives on a different plane which is governed by different rules. So now the question is can something, like love, which exists on the spiritual plane, be experienced before one believes in the possibility of love? In other words does something which exists only on the spiritual plane require the human brains or hearts or souls affirmation of the possibility of its existence before it can be experienced.

Is the belief in love a condition precedent to the experience of love on the spiritual plane? An even broader question for mankind is can we as humans experience anything on any level whether material or spiritual which cannot be processed by our consciousness.

- Before we can answer we should look at a definition of the spiritual plane. a demarcation of the Great Continuum of Consciousness that can be delineated by certain unique phenomena that differentiates it from other Planes . . . .
- www.mudrashram.com/glossarypage.html

The definition therefore presupposes that the spiritual plane is separate from let's say the material plane and different phenomena occur on the spiritual plane than on the material. Of course we have already reached that conclusion by our example of the Sun and love. Other examples of phenomena on the spiritual plane would be extrasensory perception, prescience (as in my knowledge of the content of the call about my grandmother's death), belief in God, belief in the devil or evil etc. Many of us have had experiences which were prescient or in which we experienced or saw people who have died. My wife once saw her father standing in our living room and felt him touch her shoulder. Does a perception of some phenomenon make it real?

The other part of the definition "a demarcation of the great continuum of consciousness" paints a picture of awareness which is of varying degrees and characteristics.

We would assume of course that if there is a God he would encompass the entire continuum of consciousness. He might in fact be the entire continuum of consciousness instead of the Supreme Being in Heaven surrounded by angels. There is certainly a basis for this in the present scientific theories of space, time and consciousness.

Just as in the material plane there are phenomenon which cannot be perceived at all by our senses without the assistance of mechanical aids even though they exist on the material plane. A simple example is the continuum of sound. There is a range of sound which the human ear can hear and everything outside of that cannot be heard without mechanical assistance. The continuum of colors is another example. Being partially colored blind I can readily appreciate the concept that there are some people who can perceive many more colors than I can.

So much more are there phenomenon on the spiritual plane which cannot be perceived by all men because they, by their inherent nature, require receptors which have yet to be understood on the material plane and therefore occur randomly or at least are perceived randomly. There are people who have more finely tuned receptors for perceiving phenomenon on the spiritual plane just as there are animals that can hear sounds which we cannot.

It becomes obvious that not only is the rational mind driven by the "context" of the paradigm or assumptions which are used to ask the question but it appears that one's beliefs about life on the spiritual plane may be driven by those same factors. Is our reality limited by our perception of the material and spiritual worlds as they actually exist? Is the existence or non existence of God limited by our inherent abilities to objectively perceive the nature of the real world? Does the measuring device or perceiving device define the object of perception or does the object of perception have an independent existence beyond our ability to fully perceive it?

WHAT IS HUMAN CONSCIOUSNESS

We can all agree that we are conscious of events, sounds, motions, noises, feelings, and other stimulus from the environment around us. We can also all agree that we are all conscious of varying degrees of these same stimuli. Some of us have more acute hearing, taste, sight, or other sensory receptors than others allowing us to perceive more of the reality which exists outside of us. We also know that our perception comes from inside us while the stimulus comes from outside. There are different degrees of consciousness between the two extremes of consciousness, fully conscious and unconscious. The three most recognized states of our consciousness are sleeping, dreaming and waking. We are all familiar with these states but what are they really and where do they come from. How does science explain the existence of our consciousness? The short answer to that question is that they have been unable to explain or agree on where consciousness originates or why it originated at all. One of the answers to that question is that consciousness is everything we know and that without it we would know nothing, experience nothing.

In our everyday lives consciousness can be tricky. We all have read about people who are unconscious or comatose. We understand these people to have no ability to receive and process information from the real world. It is as if we were placed in a locked, sealed, unlighted, completely insulated room which kept all stimuli from the outside world away from you. It would also be similar to the state of consciousness which we experience when we sleep. Perhaps experience is the wrong term for in true sleep there is no experience which we can recall. In fact we could easily die in our sleep and if there were nothing beyond this material plane to which our consciousness goes then we would never be aware of our existence ceasing. Here one minute and gone the next. A candle flame snuffed out. We are defined by our consciousness without it we cease to exist as individuals and our individuality is circumscribed by the content of our consciousness. We also create our reality of this world with our consciousness.

There are other ways to lose consciousness. In my case and I am sure it happens to other people I sometimes "space out". Now I think we all have experienced this state either personally or by observation of someone else who has for a "short time" lost consciousness of the real world. Sometimes they know where they went and other times they do not. If you have experienced these times of "spacing out" you will know what I am talking about. I know that sometimes when I am concentrating intensely on a legal brief or other project which requires focused mental attention that I lose touch with everything around me including time. Everything is distorted. Time doesn't move methodically but it jumps. I am here and then all of a sudden I am two hours later and I don't know how I got there it just became two hours later. It often occurs that while I am in the midst of that jump I have actually accomplished some task. Of course the question is did I actually accomplish a task which I was not conscious of or was some other power operating which accomplished the task in my absence and I just took credit for it. I have discovered recently that I do not have to accomplish everything myself. There are some things which I can ask God for assistance with and with sufficient faith in God's ability to accomplish that task and with a "hands off" attitude on my part the task gets done. That is a truly eye opening experience, a direct gift from God, a experiential manifestation of God's presence and willingness to step into our lives and provide assistance to us merely for the asking. Many of these requests are tasks which I could not have completed on my own and I am always aware of that.

Sometimes while I am driving, as I commute everyday to work for twenty years over the same route, I lose touch with my driving. Suddenly I become aware that I have travelled several miles without being aware of driving although some part of me drove the car safely through busy traffic. I am not sure where I went when that happened I just know I was not consciously aware of driving the car for that short period of time. I was physically behind the wheel but I was not consciously behind the wheel. Time jumped ahead for me and I have no idea where my consciousness was in the lost interval of time.

But the one thing I do know is that during this "interval of lost time" I was being guided and controlled by consciousness at some level which I could not perceive and had no conscious control over. Perhaps my mind was abducted by aliens or my consciousness requires rest periods when it just goes on safe mode or cruise control shutting down only the most necessary functions. This of course would assume that it has a will of its own which is not subject to our conscious ability to manage our own consciousness which is also suggested by the lost time during driving.

I think we could also agree that consciousness is necessary for existence in the material plane. When we are sleeping we do not know where our consciousness is and therefore we do not exist as individuals aware of our environment. We might as well be dead for we have all the receptive abilities of the dead. Sleep does provide an opportunity for our "personal consciousness" to recede from the forefront of managing our day's activities. The consciousness which we experience in the dream state is less defined, less critical in its perception of reality. I do know that at least some dreams are imparting information to us which we could not have become aware of in our waking state.

Another recognized state of consciousness is dreaming. It is not the sleep state as we all know because we do have some awareness of what is taking place in our dreams and can actually feel and hear things in our dreams. I have found that you can also control things in your dream and that your beliefs and thoughts if changed in the dream (even becoming aware of the dream while dreaming) can change the character of the dream. Some dreams are so vivid that we cannot tell whether we are dreaming or awake during the dream. So when the "personal consciousness" is least active in dissecting and interpreting the reality of our daily lives, another level of consciousness, with a less restrictive screening program, allows a perception of information which would not be allowed by our waking consciousness. This suggests that our waking consciousness has the task of sorting through all possible data which can be perceived by us and screening out any information which is not vital to our survival on a daily basis. This is only common sense. If we were to experience our dream images during our waking moments, while we are trying to be productive members of society, we would be unable to navigate the complex social-material world which we inhabit. It also suggests, however, that if consciousness is seen as a positive phenomenon which enhances our lives and helps us to solve issues in this lifetime then dreams must also have that function. I know they have been extremely helpful in the process of navigating my own life and have many times shown me the path that I needed to take when I my waking consciousness was at an impasse in terms or reaching a solution for my dilemma.

We should take a minute to look at dreams and how they relate to and tell us about our consciousness. Remember that we are exploring this idea of consciousness, the thing that makes us alive to this material world, as it relates to our beliefs and our ability to accurately identify the real world. The real world is being defined as the world outside of our mind and our senses as it exists independent of any perception of its existence. It was here before us and it will be here after us. It is infinite, that is cosmic consciousness, while our own individual consciousness which we are gifted is a small slice of that cosmic consciousness but still connected because it is still consciousness and there is only one consciousness. Individual consciousness can be turned on and off as easily as flipping a light switch. If you have ever been knocked unconscious, put to sleep before an operation, in a deep sleep or "spacing out" then that switch, at least to our slice of consciousness has been turned off. The larger consciousness from which we draw our sustenance continues to operate as can be seen by our breathing, heart, digestive system and other necessary life functions which continue to purr without a hiccup while we, our consciousness, has taken a vacation from this world.

Another example of the existence of a cosmic consciousness is the fact that everyone has a consciousness which is not the exact slice of consciousness which we have. Additionally it has been shown that there exists a certain context or content of consciousness which is shared by all humans. Carl Jung explored this concept in the "collective unconscious". Additionally there have been studies of plants that indicate that they have a consciousness of and resultant sensitivity to occurrences in their environment. They have an awareness (consciousness of) their surroundings and are able to change their own chemistry and behavior to adjust to it. We will explore this more closely as we proceed in our inquiries.

Consciousness therefore seems to be the basis of who were are and what the world is at least as perceived by us. Without consciousness we cease to exist. Let me put this concept another way. Without our ability to perceive reality through our senses as processed by our mind we would be nothing, no-thing, nonexistent, without form substance or meaning. With consciousness, however, we are the masters of our worlds because we create our worlds through the way we choose to perceive it. I am an atheist. I am a Christian. I am a Muslim. I am a Democrat and on and on. Each one of these, and any other characterization which you might imagine, defines their reality by their predetermined context of thoughts which they operate from, which they define their reality from. This division of consciousness into factions, parts, philosophies is taking the whole of cosmic consciousness and splintered it into camps which are perpetually at war with each other. The fractionation of thought forms can be experienced in dreams.

I have noticed in dreams over the years that they evolve and that they evolve based on my awareness of them both after and during the dream. I started having flying dreams in college. The first ones were just attempting to get off the ground by flapping my arms. They gradually progressed over many years to flying dreams where I could fly without restraint and complete freedom from fear until, during the dream, I realized I was dreaming and became fearful and that was all it took to end that flight. I could also fly through windows and doors except when I thought about a possible collision just before I attempted to go through the object and then I would be unable to accomplish the pass through. The unadulterated joy and freedom of flying is abruptly brought to a halt when a consciousness of self appears for a moment and with that appearance a concern for the material self controls the action to protect the persona which reigns on the material plane. Complete freedom of consciousness allows for actions which are considered impossible on the material plane where consciousness is severely restricted and programmed to survival mode for the persona. A consciousness which is clinging to the material plane, to the materiality of the body and its survival, is not free to take flight into the spiritual plane. Fear which is grounded in our own materiality clips the wings of our flight into the world from which we arose, the center of cosmic energy of which we are all a part.

I learned that if my conscious mind allows, worries, fears, anxieties to enter my consciousness during the dream state, when I was performing amazing feats, (at least for the material plane) then it was like putting the brakes on. The interference of the "personal mind" (which is a much smaller paradigm then even our individual consciousness) somehow interfered or shut down the operation of the cosmic features of our consciousness. The personal mind acts as a restrictive force, a repressive energy which contains and diminishes the power of the fully conscious mind. To a large degree these restrictions are a defensive system of the personal mind which can be overwhelmed by the force of the cosmic or even personal consciousness. The personal mind is too shallow, too frail, too afraid and too self absorbed to survive the infinite power of full consciousness. The finite personal mind would be completely overwhelmed by the infinite nature of consciousness if it did not have the ability to regulate the flow of consciousness through it. The resistance and restriction of that naturally unimpeded flow of consciousness through our minds is necessary for the survival of the "personal mind" or ego. The ego must be fortified with objects in the material plane in an attempt to stem the tide of consciousness which would otherwise destroy it. Among the threats which the waking consciousness perceives in the material world are other "personal minds" which compete for the same necessities of life.

This may seem trivial but in the larger context of our discussion of consciousness it is important to note that our "personal mind" and all its petty concerns, anxieties, fears, hates, annoyances and tribulations acts as a "bottle neck" for the larger consciousness within ourselves and certainly for any cosmic consciousness which exists and to which we are inexorably bound by our birthright. This is not a hypothetical for the dream state directly mirrors the psychic relationships between our "personal mind" and the rest of the inhabitants of the material and spiritual planes.

I am a firm believer in the great hidden value of knowledge which lies dormant in the dream consciousness. I believe that it reaches out to us in our sleep, a time when our material world minds are operating at a slower and more peaceful rate. Of course my "belief" is grounded in experience. I have had many dreams that foretell the future. The events have not been necessarily life-changing but simple things, things in the future which my "personal mind" could not be aware. I have made career choices based on dreams. There are many examples of inventions, musical scores and literature being born in the dream state. I always know that if I am given a piece of information in a dream that relates to my real world then I can count one hundred percent on that information being accurate. Anyone who has experienced even the simplest version of this dream coaching or communication can attest to its existence.

Dreams then tell us that our "personal mind" interferes with not only our larger personal consciousness which makes us alive to the real world but it interferes with any messages which the larger consciousness (cosmic consciousness) is trying to get through to our personal consciousness. If we make a small leap and hypothesize that everything which exists has consciousness and the sum of all these individual consciousnesses is cosmic consciousness which in turn is aware of everything at all times then we get close to describing God. The only other condition is that the cosmic consciousness must contain elements which can simply be described as love, compassion and harmony in our human language. Once again the evidence from the dream state or unconscious state (spacing out while driving a car on a busy freeway) indicates that the larger consciousness which is still operating is doing so with our best interests in mind. Likewise dreams of warnings indicate a concern for our well being.

WHAT DO OTHER WRITER'S SAY ABOUT CONSCIOUSNESS

Consciousness is a term that has been used to refer to a variety of aspects of the relationship between the mind and the world with which it interacts. It has been defined, at one time or another, as: subjective experience; awareness; the ability to experience feelings; wakefulness; having a sense of selfhood; or as the executive control system of the mind.[2] Despite the difficulty of definition, many philosophers believe that there is a basic underlying intuition about consciousness that is shared by nearly all people. As Max Velmans and Susan Schneider wrote in *The Blackwell Companion to Consciousness*:

So the new terms here are "the executive control system of the mind" and "there is a basic underlying intuition about consciousness that is shared by nearly all people". Consciousness then, in this writer's mind, is the ruler of the mind and all that it perceives and thinks. That makes sense from what we have discussed. Secondly that there is an underlying belief, intuition and/or feeling of consciousness shared by most people. We of course know this, we feel this and we sense this presence of our own consciousness. It is the feeling of life itself of being alive to this material world.

It is the pain, the agony, the joy and the rapture which we experience every day.

Web definitions

En. Wikipedia.org/wiki/Human Consciousness

- "Very similar to what Carl Jung identified as the "collective unconscious". The consciousness of every person who has ever incarnated on Earth is a part of the larger human consciousness. Human consciousness holds humanity's collective belief systems and emotional experiences . . . ."

Once again we are faced with the concept that consciousness is common to us all and in fact it joins us all. The larger human consciousness means all of us sharing certain beliefs, emotions and myths just because we are born as humans.

Reality and Consciousness:
Turning the Superparadigm Inside Out
Peter Russell

"Matter is not to be found in the underlying reality; atoms turn out to be 99.99999999% empty space, and sub-atomic "particles" dissolve into fuzzy waves. Matter and substance seem, like space and time, to be characteristics of the phenomenon of experience. They are the way in which the mind makes sense of the no-thing-ness of the noumenon.

Time and space, he argued, are not inherent qualities of the physical world; they are a reflection of the way the mind operates. They are part of the perceptual framework within which our experience of the world is constructed.

Peter Russell introduces the next step in the constellation of thoughts on consciousness by positing the proposition that even time, space and matter are merely reflections of the way the mind processes data from the "real world". That processing by our consciousness is limited by our receptors; ears, eyes, brains, skin etc. and as such we do not directly experience the "real world" but we only experience the mind's interpretation of the real world. The tree in the real world is not really green the green is the mind's interpretation of the data from the "real world" object. That tree is not green it is the eyes and brains interpretation of the data received from the tree that labels it green.

Noetic Sciences Review, Autumn 1991, pages 6–17
Virtual Reality: An Interview with Charles Tart Charles Tart is interviewed by Sharon Bard [Abridged]

"While motion pictures and television impact our everyday world by providing additional auditory and visual input, computer-generated applications are able to reduce or eliminate extraneous auditory and visual sensations, heightening the sense of realness. **Proponents of virtual reality suggest that with proper guidance, this new venture may be able to train us to sense our world differently, to ultimately know that how we normally perceive is arbitrary,** that our ordinary perception is no more or less real than any other reality we or anyone else may perceive at any time."

Mr. Tart emphasizes the subjectivity and arbitrariness of our personal consciousness or "ordinary perception" as he calls it. He further suggests that this arbitrary and ordinary perception may be able to be overcome by training our consciousness to sense our world differently. This is certainly a logical extension of the concept that our personal consciousness is determined by our beliefs, thoughts, likes and dislikes and that a thorough self examination and self knowledge may allow us to go beyond our limited and inherently destructive personal consciousness to allow a greater, gentler, more profound and more inclusive consciousness to rule our lives. We must let go of the choke hold which we have applied to our persona in an attempt to make it eternal. Our material selves have a shelf life at which time they become uninhabitable. All the holding on and hoping and piling up material wealth will not delay the date of expiration by one second. We must then all ask if that was all there was. We all know deep inside ourselves that this organic home which we inhabit is not all there is to us; we just are not sure how to contact that portion of us that is eternal that is the very essence of life which is cosmic consciousness or God.

DO PLANTS EXHIBIT
CONSCIOUSNESS

❧

A search of the internet once again produces interesting facts about consciousness in plants.

This Christian Science Monitor Article has the following to say on the subject.

ByPatrik-Jonsson, Correspondent of The Christian Science Monitor / March 3, 2005 RALEIGH, N.C.

But the late Nobel Prize-winning plant geneticist Barbara McClintock called plant cells "thoughtful." Darwin wrote about root-tip "brains." Not only can plants communicate with each other and with insects by coded gas exhalations, scientists say now, they can perform Euclidean geometry calculations through cellular computations and, like a peeved boss, remember the tiniest transgression for months.

He adds examples of the "thoughtfulness of plants" to bring the point of plant consciousness home.

"Hardly articulate, the tiny strangleweed, a pale parasitic plant, can sense the presence of friends, foes, and food, and make adroit decisions on how to approach them.

Mustard weed, a common plant with a six-week life cycle, can't find its way in the world if its root-tip statolith—a starchy "brain" that communicates with the rest of the plant—is cut off.

The ground-hugging mayapple plans its growth two years into the future, based on computations of weather patterns. And many who visit the redwoods of the Northwest come away awed by the trees' survival for millenniums—a journey that, for some trees, precedes the Parthenon.

As trowel-wielding scientists dig up a trove of new findings, even those skeptical of the evolving paradigm of "plant intelligence" acknowledge that, down to the simplest magnolia or fern, flora have the smarts of the forest. Some scientists say they carefully consider their environment, speculate on the future, conquer territory and enemies, and are often capable of forethought—revelations that could affect everyone from gardeners to philosophers."

If we are to believe this data then it appears that plants can differentiate between friends, foes and make decisions about how best to approach each one of them. This sounds exactly like human consciousness as we, some of us more successfully than others; perform the same mental process when we are confronted by friends, foes or food. Additionally it appears that at least one plant, the mayapple has the ability to plan two years in the future based on computations of future weather patterns. If you don't think this is amazing based on our current commonly held assumptions about the "intelligence of plants" then you are not thinking hard enough. Now it appears that plants can foretell the future much like some dreams are able to foretell the future because they tapped into a consciousness beyond their "individual plant consciousness".

It seems possible then that plants are also tapped into a consciousness greater than the individual "mayapple consciousness" which allows access to information from the "main frame of consciousness" which holds all answers to all questions. The other possibility is that plants have no "individual consciousness" but are only endowed with "cosmic consciousness" which is self programming without the need for any "conscious individual" to make decisions about anything that it does because that is taken care of by consciousness to the greatest benefit of the plant.

You must now consider that if this lowly plant can make decisions two years into the future based on future weather patterns, some single plants which having survived thousands of years, then if we were able to tap into that same "main frame of consciousness" then we too would have this same ability of "prescience" which this lowly tree has. The author also postulates that plants can not only communicate with other plants but also with insects. So now it appears that insects must also be conscious. Of course if plants are conscious it stands to reason that insects that appear to have much more complex social patterns would require a consciousness at least equal to plants which for the most part are not even mobile.

The human monopoly on "consciousness and thought" seems to be an illusion created by mankind's ego-logical brain which used certain assumptions or contexts to reach the conclusion that plants are definitely not conscious or thoughtful. What a ridiculous idea that is. Well we also use to think the world was flat, Earth was the center of the Universe and that the atom was the smallest unit of matter. Again we have that security system, that firewall, that constriction of our consciousness which is perpetrated by our "personal consciousness" to protect our transitory, material selves. The context of our personal consciousness is to hold on tightly to everything which gives us substance on the material plane because that is where we most acutely feel our existence. To kiss a loved one, hit a homerun, feel the reality of love in your breast, feel the pain of loss; these are the anchors which we have to this fleeting material existence which we live minute by minute, day by day, year after year until our shelf life has expired. The question then becomes does the mayapple tree know more than we do about making the most of life. Certainly we rank the length of life as high on the list of goals for each of us. We all want to live as long and as happily as we can. This little tree seems to have more of a sense of how that is accomplished than we do and yet it does not have the rational computational capacity which our brain possesses or the access to advanced technology which possesses an artificial intelligence which can calculate beyond man's capacities. It seems however that it does have access to an organic intelligence or consciousness which surpasses any known intelligence in its sheer breadth of knowledge and understanding of everything in the Universe.

You have to ask yourself how this is possible. One obvious answer to that question is its ability to access the cosmic intelligence/consciousness is more unrestricted than ours because it does not possess a brain or personality which interferes with that access. If nothing else the cosmic consciousness wants nothing but the best for itself and therefore for each fractional part of itself which resides in plant or animal, including man.

DO INSECTS HAVE CONSCIOUSNESS

———— ⚓ ————

I f you are to believe that plants have consciousness, as at least some researchers believe, then how would it be possible for insects to not be conscious? Remember our original definition of consciousness was the following.

Web definitions

- Consciousness is subjective experience or awareness or wakefulness or the executive control system of the mind. Farthing, 1992 It is an umbrella term that may refer to a variety of mental phenomena . . . .

Consciousness as we have already seen is a subjective experience, an awareness, wakefulness, or executive control of the mind. We understand the concept of it being a subjective experience as we each have our own "personal consciousness" which differs from everyone else except in those instances when you find yourself and usually another person close to you thinking the same thought at the same time. That sounds like and feels like, if you have ever experienced it, to be at least for a moment sharing the same consciousness. We also understand the concepts of awareness and wakefulness which speak to the same condition of sharing reality, processing information through our senses and analyzing it with our brain. It is the opposite of being unconscious, sleeplike or in a coma or any artificially induced state from which our minds are unable to process information from the environment and for all intents and purposes we might as well be dead.

Finally consciousness being the executive control system of the mind is a bit more difficult. The implication of the executive is an authoritative position which has power to make decisions over in this case the mind. It appears to me that after our discussions the mind is the window, the tool or the lens through which consciousness becomes aware of itself. We will leave this for further development when we talk about the Ego's relationship to consciousness and God.

Before we go to insects I think it is important to ask some questions about the mind versus consciousness. Did the mind develop so that consciousness or God could become aware of itself? Is the mind even relevant without consciousness? Do insects and plants have both a consciousness and a mind of their own? Is consciousness even relevant without a mind?

In Discover Magazine I found the following excerpts from this article to be interesting.

Mind & Brain/ Evolution of Intelligence,   **Consciousness in a Cockroach**

Neuroscientists are teasing apart the insect nervous system, looking for clues to attention, consciousness, and the origin of the brain.

To Nicholas Strausfeld, a tiny brain is a beautiful thing. Over his 35-year career, the neurobiologist at the University of Arizona at Tucson has probed the minute brain structures of cockroaches, water bugs, velvet worms, brine shrimp, and dozens of other invertebrates. Using microscopes, tweezers, and hand-built electronics, he and his graduate students tease apart—ever so gently—the cell-by-cell workings of brain structures the size of several grains of salt. From this tedious analysis Strausfeld concludes that insects possess "the most sophisticated brains on this planet."

So now we have neurobiologist stating that insects have the most sophisticated brains on the planet. That is pretty impressive. That spider that I just sent to its maker was smarter than me. It didn't seem too smart when I crushed it with a newspaper. I must admit that there are some flies that elude me for days, hiding in the house, teasing me with their flybys and generally being a nuisance. Most of the time, however, they can be found dead after having attempted to fly through the screen for a week until they died of exhaustion. That does not sound like a very sophisticated brain to me but maybe flies are the dumbest of insects.

If we applied the same scrutiny to humans we might also be skeptical as to the intelligence and sophistication of our brains. The easy ones are War, especially religious wars, pollution which kills our planet, a society where a very small percentage of the population controls most of the wealth while the rest are left to struggle for the leftovers. The seeming inability of mankind to control any of its passions, prejudices, or addictions could be added to the list of signs

WILLIAM J. PARDUE

of a brain with a low level of sophistication. In short we are a society and species, with reputedly the largest and most complex brains on the planet, which is driving itself to species destruction while holding fast to all its toys and neuroses with a death grip. The problem which we have created for ourselves is that when the ship, our planet, starts sinking (being uninhabitable) there is nowhere to jump. I forgot of course about those few hundred perhaps thousand souls who will be able to afford a ticket to the Moon or Mars perhaps where they can live happily ever after. Let's see what else the article has to say about insects.

By the way the current word on the street is that after our sophisticated species is eradicated by our own self indulgence the insects will rule the world.

Strausfeld and his students are not alone in their devotion. Bruno van Swinderen, a researcher at the Neurosciences Institute (NSI) in San Diego, finds hints of higher cognitive functions in insects—clues to what one scientific journal called "the remote roots of consciousness."

It makes sense that from an evolutionary perspective the insect being lower on the scale would have been here and therefore conscious before man but not before plants. There is more.

Heinrich Reichert of the University of Basel in Switzerland has become more and more interested in "the relatedness of all brains." Reichert's own studies of the brain's origin lead to a little-known ancestor, a humble creature called Urbilateria, which wriggled and swam nearly a billion years ago. The granddaddy of all bilaterally symmetrical animals, Urbilateria is the forebear of spiders, snails, insects, amphibians, fish, worms, birds, reptiles, mammals, crabs, clams—and yes, humans.

So now it appears that the brain or some evolutionary predecessor of the brain existed billions of years ago before even insects. You have to admit that is pretty "cool". I know, not a particularly erudite use of words but still "very cool". Just imagine that you are the Urbilateria wriggling and swimming in prehistoric seas and you are the smartest creature on the planet. The only comment I have is that they must have gotten away with a whole lot of just about everything. What a trip that must have been. Of course man now believes himself to be the most intelligent being on the planet and it has not done him a great deal of good. In fact it could be argued that the less intelligent of our species if allowed to make the rules would make simpler, less sophisticated rules. They might just propose a system which served the greater good of a larger number of people. You have to admit that some of those who believe themselves to be more intelligent than the less fortunate of their species do exhibit a certain arrogance of IQ and with this arrogance comes a "righteousness of intellect". This "righteousness" is almost identical to the "righteousness of a religious zealot" of any stripe. Both categories of righteousness exhibit arrogance, privilege, divisiveness and a sometimes condescending attitude toward those not identified as being within their tribe. Both groups set themselves against others not like them and it is this "behavioral territorialism" which we will look more closely at when we deal with the Ego and what it thinks about God and consciousness.

But for now let's return to consciousness. We have discovered it quite possibly exists in not only mankind, but insects and plants. Scientists have been unable to get their minds completely around it and there are many if not most aspects of consciousness which are a complete mystery. There are some things which we have discovered which merit revisiting. Consciousness is the center of our existence. It is not only the center of our existence but the center of the existence of everything on the material plane. Anything and everything which you, taste, smell, touch, laugh at, curse at, remember, forget, eat, read, write, and then everything else is made possible because of your consciousness of it. This includes your relationship with God. There is no material world without your awareness of, wakefulness to, or manipulation by your mind of, the object out there in reality, whatever it may be, regardless of how our mind perceives it. It will serve you well to remember that if a tree falls in the forest and there is no one around to hear it then it does not make a sound. I know the scientific answer to that question is that it does make a sound but is that really what you think. I believe that if that question could be answered then we could also answer the question about the existence or non-existence of God. Perhaps the answer to the question of God would be easier because God can be experienced while a tree falling in the forest without anyone around to hear it cannot be experienced by a consciousness which is not there. You can give yourself a head ache thinking about this so let's just agree that without man's consciousness processing information from the environment then for all intents and purposes those "events in the environment" do not exist from our perspective.

We are creatures whose universe of known quantities is circumscribed by our minds ability to translate the input received from the environment through our receptors into knowable quantities. If you put a whole orange into a grinder and turn it on, the orange juice does not resemble the orange and if you were not privy to the perception of the original orange but only the orange juice you would not associate one with the other. Your consciousness of the orange juice would not also necessarily include a consciousness of the orange. The limitations which are built into our bodies and brains prevent us from experiencing the fullness of consciousness. Even the plant and the insect perceive a much different world then we do. When was the last time you could predict the weather two years in advance and plan your life around it? I can't even predict the weather for the weekend after reading the forecast in the newspaper.

We must always keep in mind that the objective reality, the "outside us world", depends on our consciousness to make it a reality. Unless and until we give the material world "conscious attention" then it does not exist. Our consciousness creates the material world by defining it. A noise that is not heard is not a noise. A bird in flight that is not seen is not a bird in flight. A fire that cannot be touched has no power to burn. A God that cannot be experienced by Man is not a God. This does not mean that there is not an objective world outside, independent and apart from us it just means that the only part of it which we can be conscious of is that part which can be "sensed". Man's world is a fractional part of the real world which actually exists all around us. We are unable to partake of those parts which we cannot process with our consciousness.

We do know now, however, that the fullness of consciousness exists somewhere inside of us. It is that deeply hidden mystery in the darkest, most primitive cave of our being which shines brightly waiting for us to discover it and rejoin our mother ship, return to the sea as the drops of seawater that we are and become one with the endless river of consciousness which fuels the passion of the Cosmos. The only experience which ultimately matters is the brilliant flash of irrepressible volcanic exhilaration which launches us into the center of consciousness where our material selves will dissolve into the complete and absolute freedom of transcendent love, cosmic energy. That is my definition of salvation. It does not involve anything other than finding that cave and that light and it cannot be accomplished if your vision is turned outward and not inward.

We are taught in this day and age that the material world, the "outward" is all that matters is all that exists. The problem with that formula is that the material world which is gone in the blink of an eye cannot be grasped with any success. It squeezes through our fingers even under the strongest of grips much like our youth cannot be contained in a tube of revitalizing cream or vial of Botox. It simply refuses capture, eludes containment and ultimately escapes even the most skilled of our hunters. The "outward" dooms us to incomprehensible desolation while the "inward", well that is the gateway to heaven.

Now it is time to focus some consciousness on the question of why it is so difficult for ordinary people, like us, to find that cave, that light and take it as our own. Why we are unable to embrace the "soul" in us, own it and ride it to eternity. At least a part of the answer is the existence of man's ego and the related mental indicia. So let's then look at this concept called ego and see where it fits into our existence both past, present and future.

WHAT ARE WE CONSCIOUS OF WHEN WE OBSERVE OURSELVES

◆

Before we begin this particular investigation we need to take a step backwards and remember the most significant fact which we have discovered thus far. Our mind, our language, our philosophy and religions are only feeble attempts to describe something which has been at least partially captured by our consciousness and demands a coherent, manageable explanation. The concept of God for instance is a concept (and a reality) for many, which is beyond the powers of man to define or capture in a diagram, words, software program, the internet, a map, a book, a symbol or any other medium which man could possibly design. Perhaps the most egregious error which man makes is to always mistake the symbol for the object. The reason of course that he does this is because the only way he can understand the object is through the symbol which he creates. He has no other means of getting his mind around any concept including space, time and matter. The object is always bigger than the word or words used to describe it. The object cannot ever be fully contained in the symbol.

Much of our disenchantment with God these days is really disenchantment with the symbols which we have created to give meaning to our "feeling of God", our persistent "sense of God". Our concept of God is driven by, and shaped according to the context of self interest. The God most of us imagine these days is one who will not allow any evil, no catastrophes, no unpleasantness and no obvious injustices. All the reasons we choose to denigrate the idea of God are tied to our overriding self indulgence and need for the Cosmos to bend to our will so that our comfort level is maximized. Our hunt for God is driven by our ego.

Of course there is the abiding failure of institutional religion to solve all our problems or in some cases to even have their leaders behave in a manner which does bring shame to their sect. These, however, are failures of a manmade creation, religion, not a failure of God. If there is indeed a God, which I believe there is, then how could we possibly know what he knows. Our choice in relation to God has always been one which hinged on faith. Either you choose to believe, even one small thing, and then test that faith through action or you never take the first step.

I always thought that in order to believe in God you had to accept everything that your particular brand of religion spoon fed you. You had to believe it without hesitation and without any hope of confirmation of its truth except upon your death or the day of reckoning which many religions predict. That was my error. I now know that faith is necessary to test your belief. If you really have faith you will then take

97

action based on the knowledge or belief that your action will bring about a certain result. The faith cannot be equivocal it must be a total abandonment of anxiety, worry, or doubt, any of which are fatal to success of your efforts. There is always the requirement for man to do his part. As they say you can trust in Allah but you have to hobble your camel. You can trust in your cars ability to get you to your job but you have to put gas in the tank. Let's see what it was that Sigmund Freud had to say about how we perceive ourselves when we look carefully. The following is from the Oxford Companion to the Body.

"The Freudian ego represented rationality and common sense, ensured safety and self-preservation, translated thoughts into action, and repressed unacceptable impulses. Consciousness was attached to the ego but not all of the ego was conscious: whatever consciousness it possessed was largely due to its links with the perceptual system, with the body. The ego was intimately related to another agency of the psyche, the *id*, which was fully unconscious, completely irrational, understood only immediate satisfaction, and was the ultimate source of the passions driving human beings. The 'power of the id', Freud asserted, 'expresses the true purpose of the individual organism's life. This consists in the satisfaction of its innate needs.' Instead of being a totally rational being, the individual human was merely 'a psychical id, unknown and unconscious, upon whose surface rests the ego'".

So when the father of Psychoanalysis looked at himself and his patients he became conscious of certain characteristics in the human psyche which he then attached words like the "Ego" to. What his senses perceived after screening the information received from consciousness was a "mental construct or application" which was a middleman between two other mental constructs the "id" and the "superego" which possessed almost polar opposite traits from each other. The Ego was much like a middle sibling who had both an older and younger siblings who were much different from each other. Many of us have experienced this in our own families. The first born is perhaps conservative, stuffy, and very restrained. The youngest is wild, liberal, and seemingly unrestrained. The middle child, Ego, has the task of the peacemaker in attempting to keep the family unit together by searching for and providing a middle ground where the polarized siblings can coexist. The middle child understands the importance of keeping the family unit stable because his or her own identity is threatened by any instability in the unit. So what Freud became conscious of was this need for balance between competing psychic forces and a lessening of the tension created by polar opposites as a requirement for stability.

The polar opposites, the younger and older siblings were the Id and the Superego respectively. The youngest showed characteristics of total narcissism and self-indulgence as are best exhibited by a baby. The definition of the Id above included these characteristics.

the *id*, which was fully unconscious, completely irrational, understood only immediate satisfaction, and was the ultimate source of the passions driving human beings.

We can all recognize these traits in our own lives and how powerful they are. The drive for immediate gratification rears its demanding head every time you go shopping or get hungry or see someone who stimulates your sexual desires. The Id is as set forth above is the "ultimate source of passions driving human beings". What a powerful force this mental application is and it is completely unconscious. The scary part of the description of this phenomenon of human behavior which we have named the "Id" is that we are unaware of its innermost workings in our lives. We would probably all agree that whatever this mental state is, that we all enter at times, it is most likely the source of a great deal of most of the evil which we identify in this world. Robbery, murder, assault, child abuse, theft, fraud, drug addiction, cheating, lying and every other self centered act of asserting your will, "the Id's will" over another is this mental virus at work.

The passions of the Id certainly account for our irrational, blind, selfish indulgence, and callous disregard for the right of other "Ids" to the same stuff that you want. "Road rage" is a good example of the blind passion of the ego. Two individuals, usually men, who meet on the road and one suffers some perceived or perhaps overt slight to his or her person. How dare they cut in front of me like that, don't they know they should be waiting in line like everyone else. Who do they think they are anyway? All rational or civilized behavior evaporates in a true road rage encounter. It is a war of "Ids" and many times it is a war to the death. The

"Id" appears to be the source of unrestrained animal passions determined to have its way at any and all costs to society and the individual. An unrestrained "Id" is not only a danger to society at large it is a danger to the individual who is subject to its every whim.

The "Id" is something that we all encounter each and every day. The lady in the plane sitting behind you who attempts to force her way by you when everyone else is waiting patiently to disembark is driven by her "Id" to get what it wants. Your "Ego" certainly reacts to that. What a bitch, how rude, can you believe her. That is your "Ego" reacting to her "Id" which as far as you are concerned is out of control.

We are all a bundle of desires and impulses demanding immediate satiation. Impatience, arrogance, conceit, aggression, jealousy, malice, perversion, cruelty, superiority, brutality etc. are all emotions which we have either experienced ourselves or observed in others. We know that demon residing inside us is irrational, impulsive and passion driven to the detriment of all who get in its way including our own "Ego". But is it also the source of our other passions, like love, inspiration, devotion, compassion, and a fervent belief in God? Does the passionate pursuit of alcohol or drugs originate from the same psychic center as the passionate devotion to serving God as is exhibited by enlightened persons throughout history? If they are then how is it that a person chooses one set of passions over another or do the passions choose the individual? Does the individual person have any choice of passions or are we merely prisoners of those impulses either good or bad, God or Satan?

Were those Christian martyrs who were torn apart by the lions driven by their "Ids" to hold fast to their unconscious compulsions to worship a God? Are all of us who believe in a supreme deity, entity, force or organizing principal called God simply driven to that belief by an irrepressible irrational force which cannot be detected by our conscious radar? One way of answering that question would be to look to our less educated animal friends, who also possess something we would call an "Id" the irrepressible desire to seek and obtain the fulfillment of our needs. They certainly have learned to control their desires for the betterment of their species. They also express love towards to their families and other members of their species. They are able to cooperate and build communities. It seems reasonable to assume based on the ability of all levels of life to live in communal harmony, despite the existence of this thing which has been identified as the "Id'" that within that concept their must also be a drive towards passions like love which bind us together and operate for the good of the community not just the individual. Do evil and good exist side by side in this thing which we call the "Id"? Are the Devil and God neighbors? Are they brothers?

According to Freud the "Id" does not exist by itself. It is constrained by the Ego. The Ego being that mediating force between the "Id" and the world without in which it must operate. We all know that the prisons are full o f "Ids" which could not be contained by their Egos. That of course may not have been the failure of the Ego but the failure of the "Super Ego". Freud conceived of the "superego" as being that nexus of morality and cultural norms which are reflected on the opposite end of the behavioral spectrum from the "Id". It represented society and the inherent rules and moral values held by the particular society within which the individual lived. There exist those of us who have cultivated a very definite and rigorous superego which has a rule for everything and everything is a rule. There are also those who have a less rigid idea of what acceptable behavior in society should look like. The rigidity of our superegos is largely a function of the superegos that raised us. Although we do not like to admit it sometimes we usually wind up repeating and reflecting those moral values which we learned from those whom we were able to closely observe as we matured.

The other issue here for that psychic center which we are calling the Superego is that each culture, nation, religion, even race perhaps has a different set of rules, moral laws and/ or societal values which are contained in their Superego. We have those who believe that strapping explosives to themselves and entering a public place where innocent women, children, men, boys, girls are laughing, talking, loving, and doing business is a path to heaven. They believe, their Superego believes and persuades their Egos that by blowing themselves up they have advanced the cause of humanity. Those innocents who have been randomly pursuing their lives and suddenly and violently are transformed into a wailing sea of torn flesh and lifeless bodies become the victims of both an unrestrained "Id" and a defective "Superego". The perpetrator of such an act of inhumanity, at least in the eyes of the Superego of Western Civilization, is not human. It is inconceivable to most people in the world that anyone could possibly conceive of this act as heroic or condoned by any God. The suicide bombers believe it is a righteous act an act which will earn them honor and martyrdom.

The larger question becomes one of violence in general, man against man, and how warfare can be forced into the mold of "righteous behavior". If there is a God is it his fault that war exists, that the suicide bomber exists? Where do we draw the line between what we can blame on God and what we have to take responsibility for ourselves? It is easy to blame God or as the suicide bomber does honor his God by his act.

Let me give you a simple example of taking responsibility. We have all seen those people who hang out at stop signs and stoplights panhandling for money. They have made good use of the light's mandate for cars to stop and wait. They have identified a captured market and exploit it. They walk down the line of cars holding a sign and looking "needy". They glance quickly at each motorist hoping for some form of money. I have to admit there are those days when I hand over money depending on the "look" of the solicitor. There are also some days that I don't. On this particular day a middle aged man dragged his feet along as he scrutinized each vehicle. His rumpled and disheveled appearance reached out to me. I gave him five dollars, a sum which is not unknown to me for a donation but rare. Something about him made me hand it to him and his expression of disbelief in his good luck confirmed my belief that I had done a good thing.

A couple hours later I happened to pass that same intersection but on the other side. I noticed that gentleman was still there but he was no longer asking for money. It was obvious that he had been drinking, that he was so intoxicated that he could barely stand up. He was swaying back and forth as he walked, lurching one way and then the other, threatening to fall over at any minute. While I was waiting at the light watching him, watching what my money had made possible he stumbled over to a low concrete wall and proceeded to urinate. It was obvious that he was not "conscious" of his surroundings or everyone watching him or me wondering about him and my contribution to his inebriated state. Was I responsible for his intoxication? Yes on that day at that time I probably contributed to his being drunk. Was he responsible for his drunkenness? Of course he was. A failure of ego, superego and a win for the "Id" could be my description of what I observed. But whose ego and superego failed was it his or mine or both. Surely his, regardless of the irrepressibility of his compulsions, he always has a choice, his ego can always rise from the ashes and assert itself. But how difficult that must be, what a daunting task to ask of someone so far along the path of self destruction. Is it really fair to accuse him of being weak when I have never had to walk in his shoes, never known what he has known, never had to be a symbol of failure to all who viewed me. It couldn't have been his choice of careers when he was thinking about careers for however long. It couldn't have been the way he pictured himself in the future when he was young and eager. There was a time in his life when he had the strength to walk a different path and perhaps for a time he did but at some juncture he lost faith in himself in everything except the contents of a bottle.

As far as I was concerned when I pondered my contribution to his state of affairs I had to count myself guilty of a failure of my ego and superego to properly identify and react to the situation. Was that five dollars the price I was willing to pay to make myself feel better about myself without regard to what affect it had on the receiver? Where was God in the middle of that transaction? I believe that Gods part in that little drama was in putting it in front of me and making me aware of both ends of the transaction, the giving and the result of the giving. The lesson I took from that was a new appreciation of the depths of despair which people can fall into and be held captive by. The need for alcohol ruled that man's life and at some point in his past he had made a conscious decision to allow alcohol to have the ultimate control. The larger lesson was that we all at some point make a choice as to what it is that we will allow to take us over, to control our lives, to make us who we are. Drugs, money, alcohol, greed, sex, and power are all opiates which demand our obedience to their commands.

There is also a point in our lives perhaps a point of crisis in which we can consciously choose to seek divine intervention. This time may arise as we examine the landscape of our lives and find no safe refuge where we can rest our torn pride, repair our tattered selves, or grasp the hand of a real friend who can comfort us. It could be a time of economic hardship as many have endured in the last few years or it could be a time of marital strife and decay. It is not illogical that many who do turn to God for help do so when they are scared, alone, dying or depressed. Perhaps it is the only time in many people's lives when they see the benefit to a relationship with God. We as humans with our unique way of dealing with our human world more often than not need a pragmatic reason to do things. When your world is falling apart and there is no other worldly means to put it back together and no person whom you can turn to help then from a pragmatic standpoint God begins to look like at least a possibility. Besides he is spoken highly of by many people and he has been around as long as anyone can remember. You may even have encountered someone who speaks very highly of him, although you thought them to be religious nuts at the time, you knew that they believed in the healing power that a relationship with him could bring. A part of that relationship involved a casting out of demons that live in us and that thrive off of our anguish and misery. But what does this have to do with the Freudian perspective?

These peaks, Id, Ego and Superego, which lie on the horizon of the psyche, are representations of our human engineering. The Id and its relentless passions swirl about searching for outlets for an irrepressible hunger which cannot be satiated. These are yearnings and desires which directly challenge the very fabric of our cultures. Unchecked they can be dangerous and ultimately destroy the self, the society, the species. The Superego is the storehouse of culture and society. It is the baseline which we construct as a reference point to contain our behaviors and passions within acceptable limits of our particular culture. The Id knows nothing about this concept of containment and it wants to know nothing about it. The Ego as a result must manage the relationship between the two polar opposites. That management takes self discipline. It requires a hands-on management of the passions of the Id.

You know how it works because you have experienced the insistence of the passions of whatever flavor they may be and the willpower which is required to resist those passions. Whether it is drugs, alcohol, gambling, work, pornography, food or any other addiction or compulsion it must be managed consciously to avoid societal punishment for the transgression. The Ego has the reference of the Superego for managing passions. Is there a God who can help us with this control of our addictions? Is there a supreme being or power who can give us the power in partnership with him to overcome the passions which torture us which drag us to the pit of hell just to watch us burn?

GOOD VERSUS EVIL, A DREAM

When evil men plot, good men must plan, When
evil men burn and bomb, good men must build
and bind, When evil men shout ugly words of
hatred, good men must commit themselves to
the glories of love.

Martin Luther King, Jr. quotes

I t was about the time that I was considering these issues
of addictions and afflictions which take control over our
lives when I had the following short dream.

The setting of the dream was not important and therefore
was not distinct. It was the characters involved and their
relationship to each other which were of most importance.
There were two of us. I was there walking casually when I
sensed someone or something following me. When I turned I
saw a dark and evil figure with a black hooded cape covering
his body. The face that peered out from under the hood was
pointed, heavily lined and inset with black emotionless eyes.
A thin cruel hint of a smile formed the meager lips as he
moved towards me. He moved steadily towards me and I
sensed from his movements that he had a physical power
about him that was unsettling. I turned and stood still while
he approached me and then grabbed me by the throat.

I have been in many physical fights in my life and therefore that aspect of this encounter was not the most worrying. It was the knowledge that he wanted to possess me, to control me that was the most frightening. The altercation did not last long. I somehow knew that the only way to prevail in this struggle was to deprive this demon of air, of sustenance. While I was suffocating him with my hands firmly placed over his nose and mouth I could feel the strength leave his body. Finally all that was left of that demonic figure was the black robe crumpled on the ground where I had stood above him while draining the life from his form. I then saw myself, as if emerging from that same black shroud standing up and walking off into the distance. But that figure that walked into the distance walked taller, straighter and with a lighter step than I ever had before. I felt a sense of victory over dark forces. I had a newfound knowledge of how to contain evil. Suffocate the devil deprive him of sustenance. The encounter, the struggle was not a test of physical strength but one of mental strength. It was my failure to invite fear into my mind which won the battle, the physical was just an outward manifestation of the inward battle which had already played itself out and been won before any physical contact was made. The battle is always won first in the mind and then on the material plane.

It is imperative, I thought, to deny our obsessions any air necessary for life. They must be strangled and suffocated. They cannot be given any sustenance. This is easier said than done when you are held captive by your passion. If it was easy it wouldn't be such a major problem with our species. It is never easy to overcome these compulsions by ourselves. It becomes easier with help from others. Group therapy, rehabilitation, counseling and other modalities which we have developed to receive help from others have proven to be the most effective. There is also help from God. The literature is replete with references to the help which a belief in a divine source of intervention can be to realizing control over our obsessions. Is it merely coincidental that God plays such a key part in overcoming these adversities, these debilitating obsessions? Do people who allow themselves the freedom to believe in a God who can actually assist us with our problems have some advantage over those who don't allow the belief? Does God provide us with that immovable rock to which we can cling as the storm waves of temptation and passion wash violently over us threatening to drag us into deprivation? In this day and age is it even possible to reach a consensus on what is right and wrong?

WHAT IS EVIL

———— ❦ ————

> The real problem is in the hearts and minds of
> men. It is easier to denature plutonium than to
> denature the evil spirit of man.
>
> Albert Einstein quotes

Anyone who has been alive for more than a few decades
has experienced the complexity of the changing moral
parameters of our culture, of the world's culture. I was born
in 1949. In the space of years that covers my lifetime the
definition of right and wrong along with the contents of the
superego and shifted and changed dramatically. I think that
any of us who have survived this period understand that the
shift has been away from the institutional version of what is
right to the individual version of what is right or wrong. That
transition in the foundation of values has led to a cultural
evolution within a lifetime which has been unprecedented.

What was right or good use to be easy to identify. In
today's culture where personal freedom is the war cry of the
masses and the institutions which we could once trust with
guiding us to right and wrong have failed. What are we to
do? It is clear that personal freedom leads to the satisfaction
of personal desires which more often than not conflict with
someone else's personal freedom. How can we possibly reach
a consensus of good versus evil when we are seeking the

answer on a road paved with highest human goal being to obtain the maximum personal satisfaction regardless of its consequences to someone else? I was first introduced to this conundrum in Texas in 1958.

My favorite example of this cultural shift is race relations and school segregation. I had been living with my mother and brothers in Milton, Massachusetts in the mid 1950's. My father had not been with us during this period when we resided with my grandparents who had emigrated from Italy in 1913. My grandfather had come to this country to avoid service in the Italian army in WWI.

In 1958 we took the train to Texas to rejoin my father. Trains were a major transportation mode in those days and the comfort and ease of modern day air travel was unknown. The confusion arose as we departed the train in Dallas and immediately in front of me were the public restrooms. It was the signs above them that troubled my nine year old sense of order. "Whites Only" was not only posted above the restroom but also the water fountain. Once it was explained to me what the sign actually meant even my young brain knew something was not right, was not just or fair about this Whites Only culture. Of course as I came to know the South after living and growing up there I understood from where the culture developed but that still didn't make it right or fair. I went to schools which were segregated. I drove by schools which were for blacks only and they were a disgrace. Broken, torn, patched-up buildings reflecting the injustice of such a system and the disparity in educational opportunities which existed for other boys my age that happened to have a darker skin tone squatted on dirt lots like forlorn beggars forgotten by even their mothers. I didn't discover until later in High School that the Supreme Court of the United States had declared such segregation to be illegal. Segregation still persisted in the South in the 1960's years after the Supreme Court made their ruling.

The point here is the shift in the definition of right and wrong over a period of a lifetime, our lifetime has been monumental. There is no train station or airport where you could encounter that dark chapter of black/white history in this country anymore. Even the thought of that era as having had any validity on the scale of justice has long left the consciousness of the majority of people everywhere. I tell my sons that story and the stories of blacks having to sit in the back of the bus or not being allowed into some restaurants to eat and they have that same confused look I must have had when I stepped off that train at nine years old. The scenes on the old black and white televisions where the National Guard had to escort black students into schools to assure their attendance while hordes of white protestors hurled threats at them echoed a painful transformation for Southern Culture, for American culture. In 1958 segregation would have been characterized as "right" and was institutionalized as the right thing to do. Today it is seen as wrong, a painful blemish on our cultural complexion.

I read an article recently that in India young girls whose mother's are prostitutes are forced into prostitution themselves. The prostitutes being forced into the trade based on their "caste". Now this is 2011 and we have ten year old Indian girls forced into sexual slavery. Millions of girls annually condemned without a hearing, without a trial, to a life sentence as a packaged commodity in the sex trade. Millions of Indians see nothing wrong with this scheme of affairs. Is this right or is this wrong? To millions of Indians who use these women and children to exercise their personal freedom of sexuality it is a good thing. They have a well stocked cabinet of flesh to satisfy their every passion and because they come from different mothers they will never know the torment that these human beings have to endure. They will never care. Is this practice evil? Was segregation in the South evil? Is there a way to define evil which makes sense? We must however start from the beginning, the foundational question which must be asked.

Do you believe that there is such a thing as evil in the world? I don't want you to be too quick to answer that question just think about what it means. First we would have to define evil and then consider if we had ever encountered it in our lives. I think it is important that when we speak authoritatively or assuredly about anything it should emanate from a place of experience. Actual hands on, getting dirty and gritty in the stuff of real life tends to leave a lasting impression much more so than seeing the evil villain in a movie and being momentarily afraid to enter a dark room after wards. I know I have experienced evil in many forms and many places. When I have encountered evil in specific people I always feel it. It is a real visceral force which enters your consciousness and makes the hair on the back of your neck standup.

I remember once I was in a bookstore in San Francisco walking casually down an aisle not looking for anything in particular but just browsing when I came upon a man of indistinguishable age but certainly younger than say thirty five kneeling down gazing at a book. We both turned and looked at each other, or better described as became aware of each other simultaneously. Our awareness was not visual at first but physical. The actual connection between us lasted no more than five seconds. I felt the evil in him. I firmly believed that we could easily have entered into mortal combat in that bookstore amongst romance novels and bibles but instead I just passed him and to this day just remembering that day I still get goose bumps, shivers run down my spine and the hair on the back of my neck raises. That was forty years ago and it was a five second encounter with not one word spoken. I often wonder if there are in fact past lives and that perhaps he and I were indeed mortal enemies and will remain forever so. All I know is that he was evil incarnate. But I wonder what he thought I was? What did he feel when I passed him? I will never know the answer to that question.

I believe that if we stay conscious enough of our surroundings, I mean staying with the moment, that each and every day we experience evil all around us just as we experience good and if good and evil can be captured in an anthropomorphic form then God and Satan fill those roles.

I don't care who you are or where you live or how much you have or don't have. What I do care about and what we should all care about is how much evil we each allow in our lives. Because you know evil is worse than methane gas expelled by cows that create global warming who are destroying ice caps etc, etc. Evil is a clever little bastard. I mean he is stunningly smart and sophisticated. He has tricks that we cannot even conceive of to lure us into his traps where he plays with us until he tires and then moves to the next clueless victim. He must think that it is just all too easy in 2011. He hardly has to get up off the couch to change the channel and there are lines waiting around the block, around the world willing and eager to enter the pit of hell which he has decorated as a Hookah Lounge, a tea room, a sanctuary.

These lines are not just filled with the ignorant and helpless masses but some pretty powerful people can be found cutting in the front of the line afraid that they are going to miss something that their money could buy. Of course evil holds the ace of spades because he always has temptation on his side. That was a clever partnership indeed. So Satan must get very bored here on Earth because there are few real challenges to the spread of his disease. For evil is the real viral infection that will kill us all, annihilating our species and many others along with us. Forget about Bird Flu Virus, or Nile Virus, or AIDS or Cancer they cannot hold a candle to the utter destruction and misery which is spread by evil. I suppose you could say the upside of this virus called evil is that it is not a sudden death and at least some of us, although infected with it, have at least a short interval where we believe that life is grand, couldn't be better.

Before we get too far into a discussion of evil we should find a definition which we can agree with.

The Merriam Webster Dictionary defines it as follows: *a* : morally reprehensible :sinful,wicked <an *evil* impulse> *b* : arising from actual or imputed bad character or conduct <a person of *evil* reputation>

Looking at this definition there are obvious flaws. We have already discussed rationality and its context based approach which allows no ultimate absolute evil to exist outside of each particular culture, religion, nation, party, or neighborhood group. So to call evil morally reprehensible we would have to all agree on what "moral" rules or paradigm which we are using as the litmus test for evil. Do suicide bombers consider themselves or their acts evil, certainly not as we have previously discussed they consider their acts to be of the highest religious order. We certainly do not all agree that this act is not evil in fact the majority of people would consider it a truly evil act. The latter part of the definition is an evil impulse arising from actual or imputed bad character or conduct. That is like defining water by saying it rises from a spring. Not helpful at all as it completely dodges the question as to the nature of the beast which haunts us.

So this definition will not work when we are seeking the fundamental, universal, all purpose definition of evil. Let's try again Dictionary.com has this at least in part to say about evil.

harmful; injurious:

characterized or accompanied by misfortune or suffering; unfortunate; disastrous: to be fallen on evil days.

This is closer to what we need. We can all agree that whatever evil may be within the context of a particular society it is characterized universally as being harmful or injurious. That is why we all avoid it, fear it and go to great lengths to keep it at great distances from ourselves. Next we have characterized or accompanied by suffering, misfortune, disaster etc. This is a part of that definition which we can all nod are heads in assent. We want nothing to do with evil because it brings nothing that is good with it. In fact it can be postulated that evil and good cannot coexist in the same place and time. It is either one or the other for any particular coordinate of space and time. This definition still needs some additions. I think we could all agree that evil has a component which is intentional. I know that there are theories concerning "natural evil" and "moral evil". The difference in these two being "moral evil" has a perpetrator who intentionally takes action which is evil or which creates evil. "Natural Evil" on the other hand has no human perpetrator and therefore no intentional conduct. There is only a victim or someone who has suffered as a result of hurricane, cancer, tornado, or earthquake. I do not believe that a definition of evil can include a non-intentional act which requires no perpetrator other than nature. There are cosmic rules and physical rules which are easily discernible by all of us. If you build your home too close to the river and the river floods was the river evil for flooding the house or was the builder greedy for developing upscale homes on waterfront property to obtain a greater profit on his investment? If you overeat and don't exercise and these habits result in a heart attack at a young age is there any evil present here? I don't think so, although there is temptation.

For the purposes of moving forward then lets accept the following definition of evil.

Evil is an intentional act by a perpetrator on a victim which is characterized or accompanied by misfortune or suffering and whose results are unfortunate and disastrous. Evil is an intentional act which is calculated to, or will more likely than not, cause injury and harm to the victim.

Before we go any further I feel the need to make a comment about the available definitions for evil. Each one which I encountered was not completely satisfactory in actually describing it sufficiently so that when encountered it we could apply the definition and know it for what it was. I started thinking about this and an interesting thought occurred to me. Let's say hypothetically that evil is everything we believe it to be and that its manifestation in human form is the Devil. If I were the Devil and I wanted to spread as much evil as I possibly could so that I maximized the suffering and misery I would have to make evil "stealth". It would have to fly below the radar, be confused with other things like jealousy, envy, and acts of nature. The best way to camouflage evil would be to confuse its definition. We cannot effectively resist or fight something including other strains of virus if we cannot definitively separate it and identify it from other viruses. So if the Devil were clever, which we all know he is, he would confuse us about just what evil is and that is what I found in the definitions, confusion and lack of clarity. That crazy astute Devil does not miss a trick. So let's go back to the definition which we created.

When we take this definition and apply it to our everyday decisions to either allow evil into our lives or not it appears to be a simple matter of identifying this "malevolent phenomenon" and just saying no to its insistence pleas to enter our lives and gain nourishment from our conscious attention and physical participation in giving it life. But the doorway of temptation is not always so easy to navigate or even identify. It often looks quite harmless and is frequently justified with some rationalization which reduces it to harmless fun or justifiable and defensible freedom of choice. Let's take the housing crisis as an example just how "evil" was able to manifest itself and justify its destruction of countless lives.

During the middle of the housing boom here in California people were buying homes like bags of popcorn. It seems like everyone could qualify and come to find out we now know why everyone could qualify. I came into contact with it when one of my clients got a job as a loan officer with a mortgage company. By the end of her first year she was making over four hundred thousand dollars per year for completing loans and getting people into houses. I don't say homes because it was never the intention of the lenders with this product to create long term stability for the purchases but only short term profits for themselves and their shareholders.

Her specialty was sub-prime mortgages. She was ecstatic and could not contain her enthusiasm. She had never made more than fifty thousand dollars a year before and she did not have a college education. We know now that she was in the middle of a house of cards built by the banks and insurance companies who were lending the money to new homeowners with one hand and placing bets with the other that the loans would fail. Well they won their bets, made billions of dollars and the rest of us picked up the bill. Was my client participating in evil because she completed as many loans as she could so her income would go into the stratosphere? Well, was her act intentional, that is did she intentionally approve loans to people who more likely than not would default on the loan? Yes she did that. Was it foreseeable that her act would cause injury, destruction, misfortune and misery? I think that anyone who knows how to use the DVR to record their favorite shows would know that. Was she the one who created the con? No but without her assent to the con it would not have worked. My client was a perpetrator of evil in this scheme of things. If she and everyone else who was responsible for making these loans at the lowest level refused to make them then they wouldn't have been made. Does she think she was an agent of evil? I doubt that she does.

The next question is, were these moguls of finance who devised and created this debacle evil? You can bet your house on it and many people did and lost because they bet on the banks. Were they more evil than my client who participated to gain more money? I believe it is clear that both of these groups of people, who made the loans possible to people who should never have had a loan, not only allowed but conspired with evil to bring the country to the verge of collapse. The motive of both of them was the same, individual economic gain at the expense of millions of innocent borrowers. After the house of cards tumbled those responsible for it at the highest levels told the SEC, which had been stripped of its oversight powers, that if they had been more closely watched or supervised this never would have happened. My client just wishes she had her old job back because she will never make that kind of money again.

You know that evil always dodges responsibility. It never does anything wrong it just provides the opportunities and lets mankind make the choices of doing what is right or doing what is not right but that is evil. I must admit, although begrudgingly, that he is right. The Devil like God accepts the fact that man has freedom of choice. This is the only rule of war which these two accept, there are no other rules of engagement and everything else is fair in pursuit of souls. If you think about it, Freedom of Choice is the only concept which makes the contest and struggle between good and evil interesting.

I know that you recognized the old rogue, temptation, in this story of my client and the moguls. Four hundred thousand dollars per year in income and billions of dollars in profits without any risk is a big temptation for just about any of us. The temptress is always there watching us from the upstairs window, holding our hand in the park, sitting in the passenger seat when we take a spin in our new luxury car.

Temptation is in the bottle, the crack pipe, internet porn, your husband's best friend, your boss, every advertisement you have ever seen, television, radio, billboards, high heels clicking on the pavement, the sweet smooth taste of chocolate and of course every other sensory stimuli known to man. All temptations are not evil but all evil deeds are preceded by temptation. We all have experienced temptation and we all know exactly how difficult it is to resist it especially a particularly delectable piece of temptation. This is where God enters the picture. Those who believe that there is a God firmly believe that he is the one whom we must turn to when we need help in resisting temptation. Many believe that we are incapable of resisting temptation, at least powerful ones, without the help of God. The only temptations which concern us will be the ones which directly lead us to be perpetrators of evil. These are the temptations which are the expertise of the Devil because he is only concerned with spreading evil and completely and finally destroying any vestige of good or God which abides in the heart of man or the heart of the Universe. Do people who truly believe in God have a higher resistance to evil? Are they better people than the rest of us, kinder, more compassionate, more loving individuals who make the world safer, stronger and more peaceful for all of us?

I believe that we can all agree that the leading temptations for men which result in evil deeds most often involve pleasures of the flesh, pleasures of the wallet and pleasures of the Id (raw power). The leading temptations for women I believe are pleasures of the flesh, pleasures of the wallet, and pleasures of the Ego. The key question is whether or not we as individuals are capable of resisting temptation which leads to evil, without the assistance and partnership of God or some higher power which you might want to name? If we are not capable of such resistance with only our individual efforts then God finds himself squarely in the center of the first thought of the temptress, the temptation which leads us to the evil deed. If God were invited to assist us in resisting that first inclination towards evil then we at least have a lifeline, antivirus for the evil virus which has infected all of our lives, our institutions, our churches, our governments, our consciousness. I firmly believe that the powers of good and evil represented in our minds by God and Satan are real and are so powerful that we have no ability independently in our meager human form to resist evil without the help of what is good, what is more powerful than ourselves. If you do not believe that there is a force we can call evil that has spread destruction and misery throughout the world, with no corner untouched including our own living rooms, then you have not considered the question carefully enough.

Upon considering this question I queried the internet about Good and Evil and came upon a web site, Cliff Pickover, which had a list of the five most evil people in history and the five best people in history. Let's take a quick look at the five most evil as detailed by this website to see if it might help us answer some questions about evil and our ability to resist it.

1. **Tomas de Torquemada**—Born in Spain in 1420 Grand Inquisitor by Pope Sixtus IV for the Christian Inquisition. He was a great fan of a variety of tortures including foot roasting, burning at the stake and suffocation. He was credited with over two thousand burnings at the stake. He was said to be tireless in his duties.

So number one on the list of most evil is a representative of the Church, of Christianity. What a great historical moment for Satan. Do you think the Devil had anything to do with Tomas, with the leaders of the Church and the Inquisition? Do you believe that the Church and its' leadership which perpetrated such atrocities were truly representing God? If you do the Devil has accomplished his mission.

2. **Vlad Tepes 1457**—Vlad the Impaler, a prince, was best known for executing his enemies by impalement. His favorite forms of torture included disemboweling and rectal and facial impalement. He tortured thousands while he ate and drank among the corpses. He impaled every person in the city of Amlas some 20,000 men, women and children. Vlad often ordered people to be skinned,

boiled, decapitated, blinded, strangled, hanged, burned, roasted, hacked, nailed, buried alive, stabbed, etc. He also liked to cut off noses, ears, sexual organs and limbs. But his favorite method was impalement on stakes, hence the surname "Tepes" which means the impaler.

This man sounds like a man with a mission, a mission of spreading as much evil as he could with as much creativity as he was able to conjure during his lifetime. He is way beyond your ordinary evil person and I am not sure why he didn't make number one. I would guess, however, that because Tomas spread his evil behind the cloak of righteousness and God that his evil was exponential. The priests in the Catholic Church or leaders of any religion, who have defiled God, have thrown him under the bus, when they use his platform to perform their evil deeds. When they lure their victims into the safety of God's protection thereby lulling them into defenselessness that is not only arising from the center of evil but it is striking directly at the origin of all that is good.

They are the true evil ones and they should have been removed from their positions at the first instance of evil but they were not. So does that make the Church, which knowingly covered up their evil, also evil, equally culpable? Yes it does, perhaps even more so for we can argue that the individual priest was too weak to resist temptation and his belief in God was nonexistent, only hollow words spoken to the congregation on Sundays to maintain the façade, but not sufficient to partner with God and resist the temptation which was so vulnerable, so innocent.

3. **Adolph Hitler**—The dictator of Nazi Germany, Adolf Hitler, was born on April 20, 1889, at Braunau am Inn, Austria-Hungary.

Perhaps the most notorious symbol of evil in our lifetimes, from humble origins he mobilized a nation with his hatred and in so doing killed millions of innocents.

4. **Ivan the Terrible**—Ivan Vasilyevich, (born Aug. 25, 1530, in Kolomenskoye, near Moscow) was the grand prince of Moscow (1533-84) and the first to be proclaimed tsar of Russia (from 1547). His reign saw the completion of the construction of a centrally administered Russian state and the creation of an empire that included non-Slav states. He enjoyed burning 1000s of people in frying pans, and was fond of impaling people.

5. **Adolph Eichmann**—Born in March 19, 1906, Solingen, Germany he was hanged by the state of Israel for his part in the Nazi extermination of Jews during World War II. "The death of five million Jews on my conscience gives me extraordinary satisfaction," he once bragged

I can't imagine that anyone could read these descriptions and not be fundamentally shaken in their belief that there is a Good or a God in the universe that would allow such atrocities to occur. It is difficult for our minds to understand the depth of evil which had to exist to perpetrate such horrors. Such incredibly inhumane acts against thousands, millions of people are almost too much for our minds to grasp. It is the numbers which make it real. The actual torture of each individual is incomprehensible unless you experienced it yourself and even then in recalling it a certain persistent disbelief must cloud the memories. The sheer numbers are unbelievable but the fact that each of these historical mass slaughters was conceived and inspired by an individual filled with hate is disturbing.

We have an agent of the Church, two princes, a head of government and an agent of the government. The pattern appears to be that individuals who harbor such an extreme hatred for some select groups of their species are able to garner sufficient status and leadership to amplify their hate throughout a nation, a religion a mass consciousness. As individuals without the support of "the authorities" there would have been no such atrocities, they wouldn't have made the list. How were they able to enlist the assistance of so many people to assure their place in history? Did they receive some unseen help from a powerful benefactor who had even more invested in the spread of evil? Did they make themselves available for evil to enter their consciousness and take root there growing like weeds choking out any other living thought which was spawned there? I believe that the answer to both of those questions is a resounding yes. They had help from whatever powers control evil in the universe and they allowed evil to enter their consciousness and possess it. Furthermore the hatred which they allowed to grow inside them could not be contained. It reached such a critical mass that it sought expression beyond the individual and infected millions.

We all know how it feels to hate. We may hate the heat, the bugs, the noise, the pollution, your mother or father, your brother or sister, the neighbor, Muslims, Jews, Catholics, blacks, whites, browns, your life, the thought of death, God, Satan, the list is endless. The curious thing about hate is it is more acceptable and widespread in our human society than is love. Think about how easy it is to hate someone. They have slighted you in some manner, they do not belong to your political party, they are poor, they are rich, they are uneducated, they are educated and they fail to respect and recognize your righteousness, they disrespect your favorite sporting team. Listen to talk radio. It is all about hate. It revels in hating and getting you to hate the same thing they hate. Hate gives us an outlet for our frustrations, our failures, our shortcomings. It allows us to take all that pent up disappointment and spew it out on someone else. It is an analgesic for our fears and anxieties, the pain which we have pushed deep within us and which we cannot release lawfully until we can find something, some group, some individual which society allows us to hate, which is a designated target of hate.

Frequently the object of our hatred is virtually unknown to us. Growing up in the South it became evident that whites did not mix with blacks. It is still that way in many parts of this country not just the South. The point is that it is easier to hate someone if you don't know them. In order to hate someone you know they usually have to have perpetrated some act against you with the intent to do harm. When you hate someone who you don't know, what you really hate are your thoughts about them. You couldn't hate them as individuals, you don't know them.

I can still remember the neighbor girl who would come over at night to visit with her parents. While the adults visited she would get our puppy and hold it, play with it, but all the while keeping her eyes on me to gauge my jealousy, my envy, my growing animosity towards this girl who dared to come into my house and take my puppy into her arms and enjoy its warm fur and cold wet nose against her skin. It was clear that her primary interest was not in the puppy but my reaction. I remember my young heart hating her, taking what belonged to me and doing what she would with it. Hate comes so easily to us especially when we are young. There are many things from my childhood that taught me to hate or perhaps they taught me to see hate wherever I looked, instead of seeing love which would have been just as easy because it was there too. I think I didn't' see love because I wasn't sure what it looked like. I think that's why lots of us see hate wherever we look.

Perhaps instead this girl just loved my puppy. Were her looks to me just a look of pleasure that a puppy gives to a child? Was I the one who was hateful because I had nurtured so much hate it was all I could see? I do know that our individual hatred starts from inside us, whether someone else put it there or we just allowed it to grow. I do know that hate is powerful and it must be micro-managed if we want to avoid evil. It just happened that many years later when I was in college I heard that this neighbor girl who held my puppy and my hatred in her hands so long ago had died of a drug overdose. I will have to admit that when I heard that news I felt a dark satisfaction, I felt that justice had been done. That hatred still lived in me and it felt vindicated. Once hate is allowed in our minds, our consciousness and it is nurtured it is almost impossible to remove it totally. There is always some small black hard nugget of hate that would show up on a cat scan if we looked closely enough. Hate is poison to all whom it touches. Hate breeds more hate which gives birth to only evil offspring.

A final word on evil in the form of a dream and then we will explore all that is good.

THE LIONS ROAR

t was early in my new found enthusiasm for faith and
God that I had this dream. Now usually my dreams are
almost totally visual experiences for me. Of course there are
feelings like fear, exhilaration and anxiety which occurs and
is evident but for the most part the visual medium controls
and is the central mode of expression. Every once in a while
I will be awakened by a noise and I am not sure if that noise
was part of the dream or something in the house. In this
particular dream the sound became the focal point of the
dream and my research on the dream afterwards.

I was lying under a table or desk and I sensed that
there was something out there in the undefined geography
surrounding me that I was hiding from. I was crunched up
lying on my side on the floor with the table above me. I was
not moving but lying very still much as a rabbit would who
was sought out by a fox looking for his dinner. It was then
that I heard the roar. It was as clear as if I had been standing
around the corner from the lion's cage at the zoo and that
king of beasts had come to the bars of the cage and roared.
He had roared at me, although he couldn't see me standing
there shaking out of sight. He sensed me; he knew who I was
hiding in the shadow of the table, unseen, but what his eyes
could not see he could feel. He felt the fear, the vulnerability.

I knew it was the beast that I was hiding from and I noticed that my feet were sticking out from under the table, clearly visible to any carnivore which ambled by with an appetite. I quickly tucked my feet up under me leaving no evidence of my presence under the table. I knew then that I would be safe but I had to be vigilant, careful or else next time one careless mistake would find me on the menu.

I was very curious about this dream because of the roar, the lion and my complete ignorance of what it might mean. That lion was definitely on the prowl looking for its next victim. So I went off to the internet where to my great surprise I found an abundance of information about the "lions roar". It was associated with both God and the Devil but most closely with the Devil. I knew then that the Devil, Evil, is always searching for new victims. I became aware that if we do not take every precaution we will be the next meal for that evil beast. We must tuck our legs and every other body part under the desk of our "righteousness" in order to avoid his jaws. When I say "righteousness" I mean blamelessness, behavior beyond reproach. We are only vulnerable to the lion when we have given him an opening, left our bad acts hanging out from under the table. If anyone is "righteous" enough there is simply no place that the lion has to get a hold of. There is no point of vulnerability no place that can be attacked by evil because your virtue is impenetrable.

If you can recall earlier we postulated that good and evil cannot exist at the same place and same time. The lion could circle you all day long and he would only get hungrier. The lesson for me was that if evil is to be avoided in the individual's life then that life has to aim to be perfect, to be virtuous and to be God like. I am sure this sounds absurd, outrageous and impossible on top of being no fun at all. The fact is that it is none of the above, but simply an act of surrender to a higher good. It requires only a desire to be better, to do better, to make a better life and in so doing allow ourselves to be voluntarily and willingly directed in our actions. It simply involves a request to some power higher than ourselves to guide us and teach us that we may be transformed into a higher and stronger version of ourselves. We must surrender our wills to the will of the Divine. As for the fun, fun is great but overrated because it has such a short half life and requires continuous fixes, often expensive or risky, to sustain itself. Tranquility, however, even a taste of it is incredible and it lasts forever, it doesn't run out at the same moment the keg does. The price of admission to heaven is to voluntarily relinquish all control and let the divine will take you where it may. You may be very pleasantly surprised what it has in store for you.

WHAT IS LOVE

I t is clear to me that love is less acceptable and less prevalent than hate. The clearest example of that is the number of people whom you are able to safely love. Our society puts many restrictions on who we can give our love to. Strangers are not supposed to receive our love. Love is for family and friends. Love outside of family and friends is always suspect. Even love of our individual selves is caste in a dubious light. Try telling someone in your family that you really love yourself, who you have become, and watch the reaction. Love is also seen as a limited commodity in our society. We believe that there is only so much of it therefore we have to parcel it out so that there is sufficient love for those who most count. We believe that if we give it to someone else there is less for others. Why is it that we believe that love is limited? Is it because many of us received love in portions a little bit at a time so that we weren't spoiled? I can't remember my father or mother ever telling each other that they loved one another. I never told my parents I loved them until I was exposed to the 60's culture and then I couldn't stop telling them. I think I started hugging people in 1969 and I have never stopped.

One of the wonderful things about the 1960's besides the sex, drugs and rock and roll was the idea that love was bountiful and that everyone had the right to love everyone else and that there was an inexhaustible source for us all to draw from. The saying was peace and love. We often forget about the love part. The more you loved the more love there was. It wasn't a resource which was diminished by use but one that multiplied by use.

Why is it that our species chooses probably the most incredible, wonderful and healing emotion and wants to contain it, draw a circle around it, fence it in and limit its distribution? I believe that we feel the need to control the spread of love because it is not as easily controlled as hate is. We know we can hate and that we can control who we hate and how much we hate. We are in control with hate, or at least we think we are, and in the end that is all that really counts to us is what we think. Reality takes a distant second to the thoughts which rattle around in our brains. Does the Devil have something to do with us believing that we can control hate? I wouldn't be surprised, that Devil is one tricky bastard. Of course the Devil has evil on his side and we all know what a sticky affair evil can be. Just to put a finger into it you cannot help but come out with sticky fingers, like glue, very difficult to be rid of.

Love is a different animal it is not as easily controlled. Love at first sight, lost in love, love struck, blind in love, madly in love, love sick and crazy in love are among many of the descriptions of our state when love has taken control of us. This can be a wonderful emotion but it is fraught with traps for our ego, our Id, because it requires surrender. In order to be truly in love there must be an acquiescence of "yourself "for the sake of another. Hate on the other hand is the love child of our Id and Ego because it is all about drawing power and control to ourselves to the detriment of others. Love is an emotion which is bigger than us and which comes to us from a higher order with a greater ability to forget themselves or at least focus on others before we obsess on ourselves. After all love and "goodness" is essentially forgetting about ourselves at least momentarily and focusing on someone else, acting towards them with an attitude of loving kindness. It really is the polar opposite of evil and hate which always has the intent and goal of destroying, making something less rather than more, being malicious, characterized by ill will and defeated victims.

If you are currently in love or have been in love you know what dominion it can have over you. At least in the early stages you can experience your legs getting weak, sweating, excessive grooming, trouble breathing, trouble talking and a myriad of silly behaviors which you never experienced before. The World looks better, brighter and hopes blossoms when love is around. Everything in its path is transformed. Lipstick was never so red. Perfume was never so alluring. The line of a calf as it flows into an ankle was never able to capture your attention so wholly, so intensely. The old couple walking down the street holding hands, once only a pair of tortoises who you were trying to negotiate around as you raced to your next important engagement, are now endearing. Iraq, Iran, Osama Bin Laden all appear less evil, less threatening. You feel stronger, smarter, better looking, healthier, and a positive attitude now shines a bright ray of Sunshine on that gloomy trail through the dark woods that you called home. God is in the house.

I think I am safe calling love the symbol of ultimate "good" but to be safe a definition of "good" should be explored. Wikipedia has the following to say about what is "good".

In religion, ethics, and philosophy, the phrase, **good and evil** refers to the location on a two-way spectrum of objects, desires, or behaviors, the *good* direction being morally positive, and the *evil* direction morally negative. *Good* is a broad concept but it typically deals with an association with life, charity, continuity, happiness, and prosperity.

The part of the definition which deals with morally positive and morally negative as defining the distinction of terms is useless to us as previously discussed. Anything which is defined by "morality" when morality itself is culturally diverse and absolute morality is elusive is useless. Because of that we need to focus on the later part of the definition. "Good" things are typically associated with life, charity, continuity, happiness and prosperity. Once again we are faced with a definition which is utterly lacking the clarity to affirmatively identify "good" if we saw it in the supermarket or car wash. Evil is also associated with life and prosperity. Evil can also be associated with happiness, although the definition of happiness would have to be confined to some short lived physical sensation of pleasure for this purpose. I am not sure what they were thinking about when they threw in the word "continuity". Evil has continuity. That leaves us with the single word "charity" which arguably is the most succinct of all the words used to define what is "good".

Charity is defined as : Wikipedia tells us that Charity is In Christian theology **charity**, or love (agape), means an unlimited loving-kindness toward all others.

The term should not be confused with the more restricted modern use of the word charity to mean benevolent giving.

Now we are getting somewhere. Good equals charity equals unlimited loving-kindness toward all others. That is a definition which we can carry around in our pockets and take it out anywhere, anytime and view reality through its lens to differentiate "good" from everything else.

Let's look at some examples and see if we can discern the "good" from the not so good. I had an acquaintance tell me a story about her dinner party. It seems that several people were present including her teenage son and his girlfriend, her teenage daughter and her friend, her daughter's teacher and her son's girlfriend's mother. It just happened that the girlfriend's mother was a very large woman. It was also common knowledge that the girlfriend was very sensitive about her mother's weight. The conversation turned to a discussion about how much the girlfriend's mother liked sports. My acquaintance, a woman, told me that she was describing this woman's enthusiasm for sports and used the words a "big fan" and a "huge fan". My acquaintance's daughter began laughing as did her friend. My acquaintance also began laughing. Now my friend was laughing as she told me this story about how she had publicly insulted this woman whom she had invited into her home. The interesting part of the story was she did not see anything wrong with her treatment of the woman, other than a passing remark that she hoped it would not affect her son's relationship with his girlfriend. This story is repeated a hundred million times a day around the world with a different cast of characters, a different story line and different languages but always with the same laughter and diminution of another human being for the momentary pleasure of others. We really do enjoy feeling superior to others, especially those who are such easy targets.

Back to our definition of "good" or "charitable" does this act qualify as a good act, an act of unlimited loving-kindness? We all know it doesn't. Was it done intentionally? Well I wasn't there but I know that even if the first reference to "weight" was unintentional the ensuing laughter shared by those in the kitchen, with the exception of the girlfriend and her mother, was intentional and cruel. Perhaps the reality here is that hypothetically if a person has never been exposed to public humiliation or belittling but has always been the perpetrator of such acts then it is impossible for the perpetrator to have any sympathy for the victim. Sympathy requires an affinity between the parties. Sympathy requires a harmony of feelings such that a harm experienced by one is equally experienced by the other. The only way true sympathy develops is by having been the victim, by having experienced the pain of victimization. You know what it feels like and you don't wish that cold blade of blind cruelty on anyone because when you feel the blade enter the victim you experience those old wounds again as if they were freshly rendered unto you.

Does this mean that goodness derives from personal experience as the victim of evil which leaves that person with an indelible scar of cruelty which turns red and throbs whenever it is even remotely in the vicinity of "evil", that which is not good. Without the affinity, the memory of pain, there is no deterrent to the instant gratification which mocking another brings to the perpetrator. We are after all a species who calculate our acts on their potential effect on us. We know if we kill someone we will most likely go to jail for a long time. As a result most of us refrain from killing or harming another person.

Let's return to my acquaintance's dinner party. A day later the woman still did not get it. Is there any connection here between God saying that the meek shall inherit the earth? The meek are the ones that are more likely than not to have that cruel blade of humiliation thrust into their soft bellies, repeatedly and therefore under the above theory resist doing it to someone else. But does the resulting sympathy, loving-kindness for others exalt them in God's eyes? God has to be interested in anyone who is spreading "goodness" or avoiding evil for that is what he is about. The real God whatever he might be is concerned with the positive in life, with charity, goodness, love. He has bequeathed the negative aspects of character to the Devil with the caveat that we are ultimately the ones that choose between light or dark, good and evil, positive and negative, constructive and destructive acts.

We have heard the proposition that God is love. That seems credible, seems appropriate that God is the manifestation of all that is loving-kindness, that he would be love itself. I personally do not believe that God is love itself but I do believe that it is his most defining characteristic, it is what any of us who are searching for God go looking for. We are often lost and feel loveless, uncared for, invisible when we start our search for God. I was certainly taken by the Good Shepherd image. We are searching for that shepherd who loved each and every one of his sheep and whose sole job was to keep them all safe and to love them. In loving us God wants us to be fulfilled, wants us to experience ourselves as we were meant to be from birth. The fullness, the delight, the joy which he wants for us is greater than what we want for ourselves in most cases.

I have a cat and I often think that the way I care for that cat is the way God cares for us. Any of us who have pets and care for them know the feeling. You do everything for them and make sure that no harm comes to them. You watch over them and provide all their needs. God does the same for us. He provides everything which we need if we are paying attention and if we are consciously allowing him to help, asking him to help. I am not saying that everything is perfect when God gets involved but things get better according to our ability to align ourselves with the divine will. If my cat, which has free will decides to run outside, when the door is left open momentarily (he is a housecat), and he gets run over then is God responsible for that? If you are a supporter of the God concept then the answer maybe yes it was God's will. The other option is that the cat was drawn by temptation of the beautiful outdoors and was ignorant of the grim reaper which ran on four wheels and God allowed him to do that.

The shepherd has to contend with wolves, lions and other manifestations of the real world that must eat to live must kill to breed and a sheep or a housecat is just a meal. Are the carnivore hunters evil because they deprive their prey of life? The concepts and defining characteristics of good and evil become fuzzier as they move towards the middle of the spectrum which is defined by good and evil on polar opposites of that spectrum. The closer to the middle each gets the more difficult it becomes to know one from the other. We are all faced with those little choices which confuse us as to their character. Is it evil to pick up a five dollar bill and put it in your pocket after you saw someone drop it out of their pocket unaware of their loss? Is it good to give five dollars to a homeless man who is just going to buy alcohol and get drunk and urinate in public? Is it evil for a teacher to call a student to the front of the room to humiliate her because of inability to grasp geometry? As our society becomes more complex there are more and more of these close questions which when a choice of actions is made then become a direction taken which is either towards or away from good or evil. Once a direction is chosen it becomes more difficult to turn around and go back unless of course there is a crisis. That is usually when we turn around and find God behind us watching over his sheep that has strayed ready to lead her back to the herd. He leads us back with unconditional love and compassion, just like we would pick up our pet from the street after it had been hurt because it made a wrong choice.

How does the concept of loving kindness fit with the need to survive to eat? God is as concerned about the hunters as he is about the hunted. We all have an expiration date when we are born. The method of our death is left up to us in many cases. Many of us will die of un-natural causes. There will be auto accidents, gunshots, drowning, electrocution and a myriad of other modalities. Many of those will be a direct result of our behavior, our choices and our free will. If we have studied the theories of evolution we know that the basic concept is that the strong survive. Survival of the fittest is the slogan on the banner of the survivors. Each and every species which has disappeared was unable to adapt to changing circumstances in their environment quickly enough to avoid extinction. Their DNA failed to yield the necessary genetic solutions to produce viable and competitive traits allowing them to survive their competition. I firmly believe in the theories of evolution and the procession of life from simple to complex. That, however, does not eliminate my belief in a divine or cosmic force which we refer to as God which is the law which drives evolution. This is not the concept of God which we were raised with and in most circles it is heresy.

We must know by now that the old definitions of God cannot be exclusive they must be expanded to fit the growth in knowledge, culture, and experience. God can be all things to all people and he should be but he also has defining traits which separate him from evil, from Satan. God's value to all of us who believe in him is in the power to do good, the desire to do good and avoid evil. God's value to those who do not believe in him is the lives of believers who choose good over evil thereby increasing the "good" in the world to the detriment of evil. After all we all live in the same world whether we are believers or non-believers. This is not to say that you have to be a believer in a divine being or cosmic force to do good deeds. That would be foolish, however, you will recall that we reviewed the five most evil people list and now it is time to review the five "best" human beings as defined by that same list. Perhaps we can learn something from this group of individuals which will help us to define who it is that is spreading "good" or unlimited loving kindness in this world of ours.

WHAT IS GOOD

———— ❧ ————

The Cliff Pickover website lists the top five "good" historical individuals.

1. **Buddha**—Buddhism, far more than Christianity or Islam, has a very strong pacifist element. The orientation toward nonviolence has played a significant role in the political history of Buddhist countries.

We have all heard of the Buddha the founder of the Buddhism. What you may not know is that the he was also born a Prince as were at least two of the individuals on the most evil list. He was born in Kapilavastu (Nepal) in 563 B.C.E, of King Shuddhodana and Queen Maya, rulers of Sakyas. According to the Pearls of Wisdom website his mother had a dream before he was born which involved an elephant with six tusks, carrying a lotus flower in its trunk which touched her right side. The Brahmins predicted the birth of either a great King or a great holy man based on the dream. Let's remember that this was before all the self-help books on dream interpretation were written. How did those wise men know simply from such a bizarre dream that this would be a special person, did they know something which we don't know about dreams? Does the fact that the dream foretold the boy's fate suggest to us that perhaps we all have our own fates which are programmed into our DNA? Is there one path for each of us, which is foreordained if we don't mess it up, if we are brave enough to stay the course and follow the "way of life" the divine will?

The story according to Pearls of Wisdom is that Siddhartha (meaning he who has accomplished his goal) emerged from his mother's right side, where the elephant had touched her in the dream, walked in the four directions of the compass and wherever he walked lotus flowers bloomed. His mother the Queen died seven days after his birth. Following that he was sheltered from the hardships of the world, kept within the royal city, insulated from the real world. He married at twenty had a child but at 29 he took two unauthorized excursions outside of the royal city and his life changed. He discovered old age, death and sickness and on his second trip encountered a homeless holy man in search of a state in which old age, death and suffering are unknown and he had given up everything to find that state. That was all it took for Siddhartha to renounce his royal privileges and adopt the life of an ascetic, a holy man in search of the answers to the dilemma which the homeless ascetic had planted in his mind.

After many years wandering India and living a life of extreme self-denial when he was almost too weak to carry on he found himself under a "fig" tree by the side of a river and it was there that he began his meditation from which he emerged an "enlightened man". During his meditation the evil god, Mara, sent many temptations to Siddhartha including, lust, thirst, discontent and the temptations of pleasure all of which the Buddha was able to resist.

The Pearls of Wisdom website goes on to report that upon his death at the ripe old age of 80 he left a final message to his disciples; "Everything that has been created is subject to decay and death. Everything is transitory". "Work out your own salvation with diligence". His legacy was one of non-violence, self-denial beyond those things necessary for survival, and a dedication to finding salvation through personal effort.

What makes a Prince turn himself into a pauper? What would make any of us today give up those material assurances of safety, well being and the privileged life to seek an elusive mental construct which promised salvation? The answer which Buddha was seeking was the key to freedom from the chains which bind us to the material plane. Sickness, death, old age, temptation, lust, pleasure were the ties that bound him, that tortured him into a life of self denial in hopes of reaching the answer, accomplishing his goal, as his name predicted he would. Today these are the same ties that bind us and many of us still seek, with various degrees of effort, a means of escaping the anxieties, physical limitations, and ailments associated with the biological limitations of the material plane. Those who seek a God, a rule of the Cosmos, a universal energy, an immortal force are also seeking an answer to that same question which Buddha posed and answered for himself. As a result of his personal efforts, just one man's efforts, he has earned himself the lead spot on at least one list of the World's best people.

Back to the Cliff Pickover Website to the other top "good guys".

2. **Baha'u'llah**—Baha'is believe that all the founders of the world's great religions have been manifestations of God and agents of a progressive divine plan for the education of the human race. Despite their apparent differences, the world's great religions, according to the Baha'is, teach an identical truth. Baha'is believe that Baha'ullah (d. 1892) was a manifestation of God, who in His essence is unknowable. Baha'ullah's special function was to overcome the disunity of religions and establish a universal faith. Baha'is believe in the oneness of humanity and devote themselves to the abolition of racial, class, and religious prejudices. The great bulk of Baha'i teachings is concerned with social ethics; the faith has no priesthood and does not observe ritual forms in its worship.

So our second on the list is also a man of spiritual tendencies. Once again a sole individual whose goal was to establish a universal religion in an effort to bring all religions together with the goal of unifying humanity through social engineering based on universal social ethics. A worthy goal as we all are aware of the diversity of religious beliefs and the wars, killings, genocides, and general atrocities which erupt from the differences in religious beliefs. The goal of a unified religion for all people which captures the fundamental "loving kindness of God" is a sacred and glorious goal.

The next three in order on the list are perhaps more familiar.

3. **Dalai Lama**—head of the dominant Dge-lugs-pa order of Tibetan Buddhists and, until 1959, both spiritual and temporal ruler of Tibet. In 1989 he was awarded the Nobel Prize for Peace in recognition of his nonviolent campaign to end Chinese domination of Tibet.
4. **Jesus Christ**—for the preaching of love.
5. **Moses**—just the idea of "resting on the seventh day" improved the life of countless people.

It cannot be coincidental that all the top five candidates are spiritually minded individuals. They were individuals who practiced and preached loving kindness and in so doing spread that same "grace" (defined as favor, kindness, mercy or what is right) over the entire world. I didn't see an atheist in the group. I saw a group of people who were drawn to salvation, goodness, enlightenment, charity and love by a belief in something greater than themselves. It is time we learn the lesson of the Buddha "that all things which are created are transitory and will decay, age and pass away, out of this world. His final words "were work diligently on your own salvation".

I don't care what you believe in but it has to be undeniable that our time here on earth, at least in the form which we recognize as ourselves, is limited and is perishable. The Buddha taught a universal truth and made us aware that our individual existences as John or Kate or Sam or Jeremiah are but a millisecond in the grand scheme of things. It is what we believe about an escape or deliverance from that reality that will ultimately define the legacy which we leave behind us. Is there more or are we mere mortals toiling away to gather as much as we can around ourselves so that at least in that brief millisecond, which encapsulates our lives, we had some fun, we enjoyed some power. There are many people who would respond with a resounding yes to that question. This is it, there is no more so enjoy while you can. Then there are others who do not believe this is all that the universe had in mind when life was created. They believed in grander visions of creation, life in the wind, flowing with the streams, a vision of no rules and no fools.

Now when he said all things will pass away which have been created he included our "selves in that equation". We are all aware of this and we all have our own ways of dealing with it. We have either accepted this fact calmly and stoically or we are in utter fear of what it means to have this body die on us. Where does that leave us? If you are a true non-believer or unbeliever then your death is just that for all purposes. There is no remnant of you which remains behind; you have been snuffed out completely and irretrievably. If you are a believer in the continuity of even consciousness while the body disintegrates around you then perhaps as you play out your final act in this particular play you will do it with a peaceful calm which carries you into the beyond.

It is so very difficult to let go of ourselves. It is difficult because for all intents and purposes we are what we see in the mirror. That is all because we are not convinced that there is anything more to us, to our existence. We can feel our hearts beat in our chests. We can feel our lungs rise and fall as they provide life to us. We taste food, hear sounds, take baths and showers, and when we do we know we are alive. Our bodies make it all so real to us yet our bodies are only time capsules for us to explore the material world. The problem is when we try to hold on to this transitory shell, this puff of smoke, this rickety shack which we call "self". We have invested everything in this persona we call us and to see it, your investment, disintegrate before your very eyes is both frightening and mesmerizing. Imagine the poor Id if it is ever conscious of this end, it must be paralyzed with fear. We see the chain of family members who preceded us and are now gone. We have taken their places. Where we were once the young children, it seems not that long ago, and we tugged on our parents clothing and looked to them for solutions, that chapter is finished. We are now the ones looking down and the children who search our faces for love and understanding and someday they will assume our position and so on, ad infinitum. We are only here for a short time. The material plane, no matter how enjoyable it is to you, and it should be enjoyable, it does not last, even with cryogenics. Who wants to be a frozen Popsicle anyway when there are so many more interesting things to be?

I have always liked the idea of the Buddha. He put his faith to work and gave up everything he had in this world and he had a lot to give up. That is what faith is, acting on a belief without any guarantees that the act will in fact produce the result expected. Acts of faith, especially in the beginning are risk taking behaviors, mere gambles. Siddhartha took a very large risk when he gave this all up, this material wonderland, on the off chance that he was going to discover some way out of this mortal cage constructed of eternal desires, suffering and want which was built to contain our souls.

The significance of what the Buddha did with his life is important in understanding what his life meant. We know that he forsook the abundance of the material world which he was born into. We know that his life was foretold by a dream his mother had before he was borne. We are aware that he denied himself worldly pleasures in the search of a higher meaning, an end to suffering. It may have been the fact that he was sheltered from the real world for twenty nine years that caused him to have such a transformational encounter with old age, sickness and death. The two most interesting things about his life from what we read are that he appears to have had a destiny, a fate and that he had faith in his quest. He exhibited faith in the dream and followed where it led. It is also interesting to note that the fourth candidate on the list had a destiny which was known before his birth and he too followed that road which had been laid out for him, followed it all the way to his own crucifixion. There seemed to be so many of these holy men, these spiritual leaders, these wise men back in the day. Where are they all now? Where are they when they are most needed?

What was it about these three transitional stages of man which raised such a passion in the Buddha to pursue a road to their conquest? Old age, sickness and death all have common traits which define them; they all require a loss, a transition from a more desirable to a less desirable stage in life. They all represent an erosion of our powers, our control on the material plane. They are also all inevitable, unavoidable, undesirable, life threatening and demeaning. We spend an ever increasing portion of our personal wealth on fighting off these enemies of life. We have armies of plastic surgeons whose sole job is to defend us against old age, or at least the appearance of old age. Take a stroll down the local pharmacy aisle for cosmetics and find the newest and best creams, potions, vitamins and other miracles of consumerism which promise to keep you young looking forever. These aids are not "bad" they are just indicative of the battle we are fighting, the same one that the Buddha fought, but he fought it in the forest not the local drug store. He wasn't seeking a band aid treatment he was seeking a surgical removal of the cancerous growth. Our band aids help us to maintain a semblance of youth, the most desirable of human states, by covering these nefarious afflictions at least momentarily, for a night, a year until they ultimately win. When they win you can finally release those distractions of appearance, the tight skin, that unblemished complexion and relax into yourself without so many frivolous expectations.

We suffer in anticipation of these conditions because we know that they are road signs to purgatory, that intermediate state where we become undesirables in our society. They are the death knell of our continued consciousness, of our ID and of our personas as we know them.

WHAT DO FAITH, FEAR AND FATE HAVE TO DO WITH IT

F aith is an astonishing concept. It is an idea which can be tested each and every day when we awaken and walk out into the world. It does not back away or makes excuses. It does not try to deny responsibility for what it is. Faith provides a means of moving forward through the darkness, through the fear which we all experience. Faith is the key to all higher spiritual attainment. Faith is the door through which we all must walk before we can experience our own fates, before we can fulfill our destinies. You must see that when Siddhartha asked his servants to take him to the forest where he cast aside all the accoutrements of the privileged life that he was demonstrating a "faith" in his destiny. He had no idea where he would sleep that night of what he would eat or if his job would be there for him when he returned to his Princely duties. It was precisely because he did not know these things, these essential things to all of us that evidenced that he was acting on faith. Now it is clear that his faith had been bolstered by the "prophecy" but still it was only a dream, it wasn't real or was it. Real faith is similar to jumping on a wild horse and riding it at full gallop in the dark of the night through the woods. Real faith is casting aside the fear which grips us, which screams in our ears that we will die unless we subjugate ourselves to the prophet of fear and remain his servants forever. Many of us prostrate ourselves before this dark prophet because he promises safety, he promises continued life, he promises a relief from anxiety but of course he is a liar. Fear is the trap. Fear defines the limits of our evolutionary spiral towards our destiny. Fear ties us to the material plane; it controls our minds and overwhelms our consciousness if we let it. What we forget about fear is it is like the schoolyard bully. Once the bully is stood up to, is resisted his power begins to wane, because his real power is fear and fear breeds more fear whereas courage dissolves it.

It is clear to me both from my own life and from the reading that I have done on spiritual matters that faith is necessary to the growth and transformation of our spiritual selves. It is also clear that faith is not faith unless it is accompanied by action. In most cases there is a hurdle which we must all jump over which sets directly between faith and "action on faith" and that is fear. You have to know that Siddhartha was fearful when he saw the servants drive away and he was left penniless in the woods for the first time in his life. He could have called after them, had them come back, admitted that it was all a bad idea. I don't care how much he believed in that prophecy he had to have second thoughts but he had gathered enough faith around him to take that first step into the unknown.

Fate is a funny thing, we can never know for sure if it was destiny which led us to certain decisions but we do know (if we are paying attention) at the time we make important decisions, decisions which will change our lives forever, whether or not we are making the right decision. I believe that we always know if we are taking the right turn or not but I also believe that we cannot always muster enough faith and courage to take the right path for us. Pardon the redundancy but fear is a scary beast. Fear is a tool of the wily beast the Devil. He is so good at using it just at the right time, when you are tired, weak, stressed out and just finished reading a story in the newspaper about another priest who molested a young man. He catches you at your lowest, your most vulnerable state.

The lion, like the Devil watches for any sign of weakness in his prey and when he smells it he pounces. He doesn't roar first but only after he has you by the throat, gasping for air, gasping for relief from the fear that takes your breath away. The Devil of course makes it easy because he wants us to take the easy path, the sure path, the path that is littered with the soulless shells of the victims of fear. They sold their dreams, their destiny, for a bottle of valium and they made that choice voluntarily, freely, happily. Not everyone is meant to be a Buddha. Not everyone is meant to realize their dreams and has the capacity to make them real at least in this moment in cosmic history, this millisecond in eternal time which we call our lives. The fundamental element which is necessary to fulfill your dream, your destiny, is victory over fear, not just one victory but many victories, continuing victories to take you to the top of your game, to the best self that you can be, to that self which God planned for you if you are courageous enough to see it through to the end. The end is defined as perfection.

I have been afraid many times but I was most afraid as a young boy. Children are so vulnerable, so easily frightened. I am sure that you can remember how intense your feelings of fright were as a child, how they made you hide under the covers or seek shelter in your parent's bed or under your own bed. There are so many scary things in the world when you are little and helpless. You have no power and perhaps that memory of helplessness drives us throughout our lives to seek power over others, our environment, ourselves. Of course many of those childhood fears were nothing more than imaginary boogey men, hiding in the closets, in the attic or the cellar, behind closed doors in dark rooms. They hunkered down in wait, ready to spring out of the void and eat us. It seems that some adult fears have that same consistency as our childhood dreams, more vacuous than substantive, more imagined than real. I remember living in my grandmother's house and having to reach around the door frame into the room which was pitch black to turn on the light. I always thought that some ghoul was going to grab my hand and pull me in. Every time it reached around that door jamb I thought it would be my last but it never was, I was never grabbed.

The child's excuse for being so fearful is innocence, ignorance. We are most afraid of the unknown and children know far less about how the world operates than adults.

To a child everything is scary and can have unknown consequences. Children have fewer remedies to meet their fears. They can hide under the covers or call for their parents or just be very quiet and hope that the scary apparition will not notice that they are present. When you consider fear as an adult it is still real but it is always fear about the future. The example is you go wilderness camping. You might be afraid that you will get lost and then you do. The state of being lost, which was a possibility in the future when you were worrying about it, is now the present. While you are lost in the present tense you are now worried or fearful about not being found, another possible future event. As adults our fears are based on what might occur in the future. Many of those projections or anticipations of future events never occur but it does not keep us from being fearful about their possibility.

I see many people now, in 2011 who are afraid, adults, many who have never been afraid before now. They are afraid because the reality which they thought they knew and had some control over slipped away or was it revealed itself to be of a distinctly different character than they expected. They are afraid because the nightly news makes them fearful; the loss of their jobs and homes makes them scared, the frightened look in their loved ones eyes pierces their breast deflating the supply of courage which they stored there. It is a fact that humans regardless of race, gender, or age display a universal facial expression which we can all immediately identify as fear. The purpose of that universal "red flag" is to warn the rest of us that there is something out there in our environment which is potentially harmful to all of us. Let's take a detour to discover something about fear and how it works in all of us, because overcoming fear is often the first step to our individual evolution and was certainly a key element in the evolution of our species.

On the Discovery Fit and Health Website they give a good general description of fear.

Fear is a chain reaction in the brain that starts with a stressful stimulus and ends with the release of chemicals that cause a racing heart, fast breathing and energized muscles, among other things, also known as the fight-or-flight response. The stimulus could be a spider, a knife at your throat, an auditorium full of people waiting for you to speak or the sudden thud of your front door against the door frame.

We all know fear. We all know that it keeps us from doing many things which other people can do and that we need to learn to do to grow, to evolve. Siddhartha could not have evolved into the Buddha if he had succumbed to his fears for his personal safety and well being. Martin Luther King would never have become the Icon of freedom and courage for the oppressed if he had failed to overcome his fears for his own personal safety. We know Mr. King had faith in God and that God had given him a path to follow, a destiny to secure and he did. Jesus would never have made the impact he has on the entire world if he had allowed his anxieties about his fate to interrupt his works on this earth. The Wright Brothers would never have left the ground if their fears for their own personal safety had held sway over them. Almost any individual who raises above the restless mass of humanity, because of the "grace" which they left behind, which they spread over the earth and which continues to influence future generations, has conquered fear before fulfilling their destinies.

The process of creating fear takes place in the brain and is entirely unconscious. There are two paths involved in the fear response: The **low road** is quick and messy, while the **high road** takes more time and delivers a more precise interpretation of events. Both processes are happening simultaneously. the Discovery Fit and Health Website

The example is it is late at night and you are alone in your house. You hear a trashcan crashing over in the backyard. You hear the door rattle. The low road, quick fix is for the brain to register the potential existence of danger which in turn triggers the "fight or flight" response found in all animals. The low road is completely beyond our control in regards to what we experience. The typical symptoms are; heart rate and blood pressure increase, veins in skin constrict to send more blood to major muscle groups, pupils dilate, blood glucose levels increase, muscles tense ready for action, non-essential systems shut down and smooth muscles relax. We have no control over this transformation of our physical and emotional state at its inception. The high road includes the same symptoms and it is happening simultaneously but it continues to compare the noises which were heard from outside with our experience of those same noises and factors. You notice that a strong wind is gusting and the back door latch has been broken which causes it to bang when the wind blows. You remember last year the neighbors had trouble with raccoons coming at night and overturning their trash cans. Your body starts to calm as you put these pieces together as you compare the present with the past to determine the "danger" which exists.

So fear serves a basic function in our world, survival.

If we couldn't be afraid, we wouldn't survive for long. We'd be walking into oncoming traffic, stepping off of rooftops and carelessly handling poisonous snakes. We'd be hanging out with people who have tuberculosis. In humans and in all animals, the purpose of fear is to promote survival. In the course of human evolution, the people who feared the right things survived to pass on their genes. In passing on their genes, the trait of fear and the response to **it** were selected as beneficial to the race. the Discovery Fit and Health Website

I am sure that many of you can recall times when fear steered you away from danger. Times when you felt the hair stand up on the back of your neck, the heart rate accelerate and the sound of blood rushing in our ears. What was your reaction to this inescapable rush of emotions and physical symptoms which prepared you to fight of flee. Did you panic and suffer because you failed to choose the appropriate option, did you freeze, or were you able to think clearly, let the high road complete its task, and make an appropriate decision. We all know that in this era of economic blight there are many things which scare us, make us fearful which are not physically threatening, at least immediately on a life or death basis. There are bills that cannot be paid and the threat of collection calls, there are loved ones who become depressed and drag themselves around all day, all week, all year not able to pull out of the dizzying spiral which they have fallen into. There is the unexpected loss of a job on Friday morning when you just purchased a house or new car or just need the job because you need to pay your bills. All of these factors which are present on the social landscape create fear. They could just as well be a hungry lion because the level of anxiety and fear which they create is equal to that experience of our ancestors trying to stay alive on the African savannahs. The environment in which we exist in 2011 is as dangerous and scary as any landscape which our progenitors faced with spear and shield.

I believe that "faith" is something larger than ourselves and is a key to overcoming and coping with the fears that are so pervasive today. The fear today is of a different caliber then anything that I have previously seen in my lifetime. It is a fear which appears to have no end, no solution at hand, because it is part of the fabric of our society. We have been taught to fear not just the lion stalking us but, riding bikes without helmets, the neighbor next door that talks to children, the Taliban, Iran, Iraq, Syria, North Korea, China, Russian, Communism, Muslims, Aids, Cancer, TB, Heart Attacks, Liver damage, alcohol, cigarettes, candy, fast foods, global warming, nuclear energy, coal, earthquakes, tsunamis, hurricanes, prescription drugs, illegal drugs, autism, Nuestra Familia, Mafia, Bloods, Crips, Bad Cops, Crooked politicians, lawyers, doctors, mechanics, banks, churches, priests, pastors, pit bulls, and on and on. There is an endless list of "things to be aware of, afraid of" which we should be anxious about and which can cause us to fear for our continued well being is overwhelming. We are on high alert at all times, there is no place other than the sanctity of our homes which seems safe anymore and for many that is the least safe of places. How many of these possible threats actually rise to the level of inflicting harm on us personally or someone we know? The answer would be very few but it only takes one that you read about in the newspaper or see on television or who lives down the street to create the perception that it is a possible threat in your life as well.

Can faith in some power higher than ourselves as individuals help to alleviate some of that fear, that anxiety? The answer for those who are capable of generating enough faith to move one step forward and test the theory of faith is yes it can and does provide peace in times of turmoil. Faith in a higher power, a divine law, a universal truth, gives us an inner strength, a directional certitude which we could not have acting alone. The surprise is that once you have started down this path of "faith" and your skepticism is turned down low enough to allow the freedom to "try" something different than what is not working anymore in your life you will be delighted at the results. At first you will be perplexed at the results which faith bestows on you and you will most certainly pass them off as mere coincidences but after a longer trial period within which the infallibility of the "power of faith" demonstrates itself to you belief will begin to sprout a tender shoot. You must however drop the skepticism long enough to consider the possibility of the existence of a power greater than you that is available to help you when you need help. This freedom to explore an issue which you dismissed years ago as mere nonsense is essential. If you cannot allow yourself that freedom of choice to experiment then you are doomed to your own resources which are limited and fallible. Of course it sounds crazy, Jesus freaks, religious fanatics, mystics, snake handlers are all part of the vision which we conjure when we talk about this. The answer, however, is not in the old myths, although they give hints of what might be there they have become lost in their own rhetoric, their own self-importance where the path has become more important than the goal. The point of contact is between you and a force that is greater than you, knows more than you, can see around corners which you cannot see around and which has a plan for you for all of us. We have to be courageous enough to allow this power to arise in us, to grow towards the light. Open-mindedness is essential.

The dynamic interplay of fear, fate and faith are important in how our lives turn out. Do we allow fate to take us to the destination which is meant for us or do we succumb to the numbing effect which fear has to immobilize our action centers? Do we freeze up and fail to take action necessary for us to move forward towards our destiny and as a result we remain in a quagmire of self doubt and self loathing because we know what we have failed to do? Are we continually

that child reaching around the corner in the dark to turn
on the light all the while fearing that we will be dragged
into the room by some evil force? There is no doubt that we
all experience fear, sometimes on a daily basis and that fear
weakens us, saps our resolve, dissolves our confidence, and
steals our rightful place in the cosmic scheme of events. It
also makes the world a scarier place than it actually is.

The easy solution is to turn to alcohol, drugs, sex,
pleasure, work, food to ease the pain that haunts us. We are
haunted when we fail to fulfill our destinies. Sometimes it is
an uneasiness which we cannot shed. Other times it is a dark
pall which hangs over everything which we do, a depression.
Experiments have shown that an individual under stress has a
lower IQ score than the same individual who is not. Fear and
stress affect our ability to cope to make important decisions.

Others can see it in our faces, our postures, the way we
relate to them. The homeless gentlemen to whom I gave
five dollars and who I later saw staggering drunk, publicly
urinating was in pain. All the alcohol in the world was not
going to ease his pain. All the sex in the world or drugs
or money is never enough to fill that painful void which
is created by our failure to discover and move toward our
destinies. Being alive is being in the flow of life, merging
with the current. The second we are born into this world we
enter the stream of life, a river of consciousness, of energy
from which we will not depart until we die. The force of that
life energy which we witness all around us, in every living
thing including the earth we walk on sweeps us away into the

middle of the current where we move towards our destiny our home, the place where we know we were meant to be. The restlessness, boredom and general ennui which we all experience comes from being away from that home. When I think about that place that home I hear the words to the John Denver song, "Take Me Home Country Roads". "Take me home country roads to the place where I belong".

I believe that we each have a place where we belong and we are programmed to reach our home during this life of ours. If, however we fail to surrender ourselves to that flow, that current of fate then we will linger in the backwaters forever restless for the place where we belong. We must also be sensitive to those subtle clues which we are given which tell us when we are headed in the right or wrong direction. It is like that feeling when you are leaving the house and you know something is wrong, something is being forgotten. You then discover later that you left your keys or wallet at home. You were warned but you failed to take the time and stop to find out what it was that was missing, that was out of place. That is how our warning system for our life choices operates, subtle clues, a hint here a feeling there, always felt but not always acknowledged or carefully considered. We all have the built in GPS system which is ready to take us to our "homes" we just fail to recognize its existence and subsequently its importance to staying on track.

We voluntarily choose, as we proceed with our lives, to be an active participant, a willing traveler on the current of life or we can shrink back and let fear cripple us. Anytime we remove ourselves from the mainstream of life, from the flow of the current which runs through us and directs our every move then we suffer for it. Fear is not only a necessary warning which helps us to survive but it is also a deadly poison which can crucify us on the cross of inaction, self doubt and indecision. We are no longer floating on the current of destiny but bobbing in the murky tide pool of depression, remorse, anxiety, and addiction. We are lost. We are floundering, barely keeping our heads above water.

One of the most impressive characteristics of the younger generations is their assault on fear. They have cut new paths through the steamy jungles of fear by going faster, higher, deeper, steeper, and stronger than prior generations. Bigger mountains, giant waves and faster cars are all just some examples of how fear has been overcome by minds not yet numbed by failure or the perception of future failure or personal harm and conquered what was once the unconquerable. I remember when I was young I was not going to be stopped by anything least of all fear if there was something that I wanted to do. I survived that as my youth endowed me with a sense of invulnerability which shielded me against all harm and kept me in the mainstream of life. As we get older that fearlessness begins to be eaten away by the experience of loss or harm which has occurred along the way and dulled the sharp edge of courage or recklessness which inhabited our younger souls. I had a dream about fear and its ability to confound and paralyze us.

THE BMX RIDER

I have been an attorney for almost twenty years. I was not always a lawyer but had two different lives before embarking on this one. I have however been a lawyer longer than any other career and I have become accustomed to doing this job. I often consider once again changing careers but at sixty two there are other factors which need to be considered. That is just another way of saying that I know it is time to make a change. I can feel the cogs turning and the mindset switching gears as the flow of my life takes yet another turn and the stream seems to be widening and slowing down. Now how to get from being a career professional who has invested twenty five years in the profession and education to the profession to some new endeavor? Fear is there of course whispering in my ear, you are too old, you don't know how to do anything else and besides why even try. It was then that I had the BMX dream.

I had been walking and I came to a ranch style home at the top of a hill. It had a narrow concrete walkway around the perimeter of the home which I followed. I was travelling trying to get to some destination which was not made clear to me in the dream. As I walked around the walkway I turned the corner to the far side of the house. It was then obvious that the home rested at the very edge of a deep crevice. Looking across the abyss there was another landmass approximately fifty feet across open air with no means of crossing from the sidewalk, which I remained perched on, to the land on the other side. I knew that my destination lay on the other side of the yawning empty space just as I knew I had no way of getting over to the other side. I noticed, as I pondered my plight, that my briefcase was sitting on the sidewalk at the very edge where it dropped off into the void. I thought it was very curious that my briefcase, which always accompanies me into court, was just sitting there on the edge. It was when I was thinking how hopeless it was to get to the other side that a young man on a BMX bicycle went flying over the canyon. As he reached the mid-point he looked down at me and took his hands off the handlebars and put them in the air as if taunting me, showing me how easy it was to make that leap. Despite my doubts that he would make the jump I saw him land perfectly on the other side and be greeted by a number of other people waiting for him. He looked back at me and waved me over and looked at my briefcase sitting on the edge and I knew I could not take the briefcase with me it would have to stay behind.

I take these clairvoyant dreams, dreams of extreme clarity which I always remember in the morning, very seriously and I always search for the message. The message was clear here. I had come to yet another crossroads, a place where fear had to be overcome and I had to make a choice based on "faith" or on "fear". Although the fear can serve the very important function of keeping us out of harm's way it can also keep us from following our destinies, from becoming the highest and best that we are able to become. Although we may all have our "destinies" already planned it does take some effort to make them happen. If your destiny is to be a doctor you will have to attend and graduate medical school. Regardless of your fate there will be certain actions which are required of you to manifest that fate, that destiny. If you fail to participate, to pull your weight, to avoid getting lost then you will certainly roam aimlessly, listlessly and without direction until the day you no longer breathe this air or walk this earth. You can wait at the bus stop, see the bus arrive but unless you get on the bus you will not get to your destination.

WHAT IS FATE,
WHAT IS DESTINY

F rom Wikipedia we obtain the following guidance as to
these two terms.

Destiny is seen as a sequence of events that is inevitable and unchangeable. Although the words are used interchangeably in many cases, fate and destiny can be distinguished. It depends on how narrow or broad the definitions are. Broadly speaking, fate is destiny. Narrowly and to be more accurate, traditional usage defines **fate as a power or agency that predetermines and orders the course of events**. Fate defines events as ordered or "inevitable". Fate is used with regard to the finality of events as they have worked themselves out; and that same sense of finality, projected into the future to become the inevitability of events as they will work themselves out, is Destiny. In other words, **fate relates to events of the past and is proven to be true and unalterable, whereas destiny relates to the probable to almost certain future**. Note that it is only almost certain and not absolutely certain, allowing for change to occur.

So let us clarify what is being said here. You have to admit the concept of fate and destiny is interesting for all of us. Do we have any control over how our lives are going to turn out? Is there some foreordained plan for us that is unalterable? If we were to reference the Buddha's life we could certainly say that his "fate" (his life as we looked back on it) was foretold by his mother's dream. If in fact the tale of his life is accurate then there is no denying that there was some predestination going on. Before his birth it was foretold in his mother's dream that he was going to be either the greatest King or the greatest Holy Man who ever lived. The story of Jesus had the same prophetic qualities as the return of the messiah was foretold in the Old Testament and of the course the Bible has many tales of prophecies which came true. In a religious context prophecies or tales of predestination were directly related to the power of God. It was God who created your fate who planned your destiny. Of course the definition of fate as set forth above would indeed require some prescient force or power which rules over all of our lives.

As set forth above fate is; fate as a power or agency that predetermines and orders the course of events. What else is that other than a divine rule, a cosmic manager or an omniscient software program which organizes and plans events in the universe for persons that have not even been born yet, sometimes decades before, perhaps millenniums before? Do you feel that, a sense of purpose, a movement towards your own center, a rushing of intensity of feeling as we near our "homes"? Or are you feeling the loss of purpose, a lack of inspiration, a cry for understanding, a need to reach out and understand? We all feel the life in us and in our clearer moments we sense a direction. Our failure arrives when we cast the feeling aside, disrespect the inclination, ignore the intuition. After all we are very busy and very important. There are many other things which we must do that are significantly more critical then listening to the song of our souls. There is such a great new movie just out. The symphony is in town. American Idol is on. Poker sounds good. Introspection and focused thought on our natures does not sound like fun. It just sounds boring, dull, lame, and not likely to lead to anything worthwhile. Poor us, how shallow we are becoming, how far from our source have we wandered. How much do we really care anymore? How much effort are we willing to expend for only the probability of success of attaining our goal?

Life is meant to be lived in the moment, seize the day, make the most of every minute and by all means enjoy yourself even if it makes you miserable. Satan has a quick mind, a persuasive tongue and he knows where you live and what you dream. He knows what you desire and what he has to offer you. He understands where the fork in the road is and if you are keeping your eye on the road so that you know which road to take. Of course if he sees that you are not paying attention he is more than willing to lend a helping hand, to steer you in the wrong direction with enthusiasm. He knows when your heart is broken and lying in a thousand pieces. He knows that by sustaining that broken heart, those shattered dreams, the sense of loss that those pieces will never return to the fullness of your heart again and he has his victory, he has captured your soul. He dances to the sound of your anger, your hatred, and your unforgiving nature because it empowers him; it fills him with a lust for your soul which rises to an orgasmic delight in your desperation.

He knows, however, that free will means that an individual can at any moment change direction, acknowledge the bonds which tie him, and choose to move towards the light, towards your "righteous destiny". It is a great folly to underestimate the evil in this world for it exists whether you acknowledge its existence or not. It is breathing down your neck. It is watching you for signs of weakness but so is God or goodness or the cosmic divinity or rule. The presence of all things good and positive is also within your reach. To grasp that "Godness" requires only an outstretched hand, a humble orientation and a grateful heart. Grasping your fate and holding on requires courage born of faith in a power greater than ourselves. I am not saying this path is easy, it was Siddhartha's path. It is a hard and difficult road paved with uncertainty, self-doubt, failure, resistance from others and it is always travelled alone, that is alone except for that divine power which is available for assistance if requested. Without the power and direction which a "God" gives us this path is beyond our abilities to navigate, to conquer. After all our individual power is miniscule, almost an afterthought. We imagine that we can control all things that with our sheer will power there is no obstacle which cannot be overcome. Time, however, reveals that misconception because with time comes experience and the flow of life which eventually brings an equalizing event into all our lives such that we have a moment in which our perspective will change forever. Our

Achilles heel will be pierced and our imagined invincibility exposed. We are not the rule makers of the universe we are its children and just like all children we sometimes overestimate our own powers.

I remember when I was young my grandmother would send me letters addressed to William J. Pardue ESQ. When I was growing up I was always told that I should be a lawyer, however, I waited forty two years for that to happen and it just happened by coincidence, with not much planning. Was that predestination? When I first learned that the Esquire suffix was used by attorneys I wondered if my grandmother was trying to tell me something or was it just because she worked as a cook for a wealthy attorney where she saw the initials on his letters and thought they were impressive. I never got a chance to ask her. Either way it turned out to be my fate and my grandmother had a sense that it was my destiny so the powers at work in the universe perhaps used her to direct me.

What difference would it make to us if we suddenly learned through objective evidence produced through scientific inquiry that we all had a destiny at birth? The first response would be that if we had a destiny then we would want to know if it was an absolute destiny or a probable destiny which we were able to alter during the course of our lives. The above definition of destiny defines it as a probable outcome but it does not become an absolute outcome until it is in the past. At that point in time, in the past, it is in the context of this definition "fate". Upon further thought it would occur to us that unless we knew in advance what that destiny was we would have no idea of why or how we would want to change it. Typically we want to change things to make them more closely coincide with our own ideas of what we should be doing with ourselves. It would also not allow us to live more anxiety free because we could imagine our destiny to be something completely unacceptable, sad, or depressing. Although we could with equal clarity imagine it to be perfect, joyful, delightful and enlightening. But we can do that now without knowing what our destiny is.

What if all those dreams of predestination or of a prescient nature were not dreams of fate but dreams of possibilities for destinies? In other words Siddhartha's mother's dream about his birth and the interpretation by the scholars of that day may have been a possible blueprint for a specific destiny. Such a blueprint would require a builder to make it one's fate, wouldn't it? Was Siddhartha aware of that dream, had he been told by members of his family, his household that this was the plan for his life; this was who he was to become. Who sent that dream? Who was it that wanted to influence this particular individual out of all the individuals who had taken a breath of air here on earth? So the possibilities appear to be destiny propels us inexorably to our fate which creates the character; or destiny is an idea (destination) which man allows taking root in his consciousness and it drives the man to create his fate. Are we the data being fed into the program or are we the program dependent on the data for a result. If we believe that we choose the destiny by choosing the idea which we allow to grow in our minds then we would ask the following questions.

The question then is if they are cast in concrete before we have even taken a breath then why do we have to try at all, doesn't it just happen regardless of what we do or do not do? To answer we need to refer back to the definition of "destiny". We must keep in mind when considering "destiny" that it is complex notion composed of intricate details and events which must occur at certain times and places over the course of your life. It is also evident that other people's destinies have to coincide at certain critical time/space locales with ours in order to fulfill an individual's destiny. It is not driving from your house to the grocery store to buy some bananas. It is a destination without roadmaps, trails or compasses involving thousands of people whose schedules have to be coordinated so that a precise time/space moment, millions of these moments with the key players take place.

Destiny, when defined on a grand scale, is equivalent to fate, however, when taking a closer look its definition is somewhat different; fate relates to events of the past and is proven to be true and unalterable, whereas destiny relates to the probable to almost certain future. Note that it is only almost certain and not absolutely certain, allowing for change to occur. This can be seen in our common language usage. Let's look at some real life examples of prophetic dreams or dreams of predestination. There are some interesting dreams to explore and with that exploration we may be able to better distinguish and discuss what these concepts actually mean to our lives.

FAMOUS PREDESTINATION DREAMS

President Lincoln's dream of his assassination:

A few days before his assassination President Lincoln told his wife about a dream which he had some ten days before. He heard sobbing and people mourning and grieving, a large number of people. He got out of bed at the Whitehouse and proceeded to the East Room. Along his way there he was unable to see any of the mourners he could just hear them. He told her he felt a death-like pall surround him. When he arrived at the East Room he saw a body wrapped in funeral attire with the face covered. He inquired of the guards posted nearby as to who had died, they responded, The President.

President Lincoln had numerous prophetic dreams especially during the Civil War and he took them all seriously. So this dream of assassination was not the first and it is interesting that based on his history and knowledge of such dreams he failed to take sufficient precautions to prevent his possible assassination. What does this particular dream tell us about predestination? Number one it tells us that there is some information which we can access through our "dreams" which we are unable to access through our normally conscious state. Secondly the information received by Lincoln in this particular dream foretold events in the future, approximately two weeks in the future. Thirdly the exact location of the assassination was not described but only the ultimate fact "death by assassination" was disclosed in the dream. The details of the assassination attempt seem to have been absent. The question then arises as to whether or not President Lincoln took any additional precautions to avoid assassination or did he merely relay the dream to his wife disbelieving its prophecy. The other question which has to be asked is if he had taken precautions could he have avoided the assassination or did the dream already reveal and contain within itself his failure to take precautions despite the warning. The other important question has to be whom or what was warning him or making him aware that his life was in danger. The question we are left with in this dream is, Was President Lincoln capable of using the information in the dream to avoid assassination? If we return to the prophecy that some child will one day be a Doctor that includes by implication the expenditure of the requisite effort to reach that goal. In President Lincoln's case it was a lack of effort in protecting himself which resulted in his death. We cannot say it was a surprise. We can say he did not know the exact day, time, place and method but neither does the young aspiring doctor know by what academic route he or she will attain her destination. The other possibility is that President Lincoln took the dream at face value and apparently believing in dreams as he did he felt it was unavoidable that it was his destiny and he could not change the future which had been prophesized. Did he let that dream thought dictate his future because he felt he had no real choice of entertaining another contrary thought? What is done is done, was that his operative thought when it came to this historic event and the dream that led to it.

The question then arises as to whether in the context of fate and destiny, whether or not there are plans in progress evolving with the circumstances and choices of each individual or are they completely and finally unalterable and unavoidable. President Lincoln's dream was about his death, a death to occur in the future. The dream arose from his unconscious and it could have been either a warning or a "final notice" of eviction from this life. I can't help but think about those times when I have been leaving my house and I have a vague but nagging sense that something is not right. I am not sure what it is but something is wrong. If I ignore that feeling, that sense of discomfort then I have chosen one path and if I chose to take some time to attempt a mental inquiry into that sense of disharmony then I have chosen a different path. There are occasions when I am in too much of a hurry and too much on my mind when I recognize the uneasiness but do nothing about it. There are other times when I slow down and take time to try to locate the source of my uneasiness. Every time that I have left without taking heed of the warning I have later in the day perhaps minutes perhaps hours become aware of what caused the uneasiness.

It could have been a forgotten file left at home needed for court, or a wallet, watch, money, or any of a dozen things which needed to be tended to before I left that morning and I failed to do so. The flipside of that is that every time I took the time to find out what was causing the sense of disharmony I discovered what it was and remedied the situation before leaving. This simple example relates to Lincoln's dream and what he did in reaction to it. His dream was even clearer than my intuitive prompting but it appears that he ignored its warning. Based on this simple comparison I would have to conclude that the dream, the sense of uneasiness were warnings which if heeded could have averted a problem in the future.

It also appears evident that our consciousness is focused on our survival and analyzing all data flowing to it from the environment in order to categorize the dangerous from the helpful. I also assume that my unconscious has the same goal, my survival. If that simple fact is true then it seems more likely than not that the prescient dream and the intuition are both in the form of warnings. Warnings which are meant to keep us safe, if we pay attention to them. But before becoming attached to that perspective let's look at other famous prescient dreams. We must also keep in mind the source of our dreams because that is where we are really going. If they are found to be of a helpful nature giving us guidance then where is that guidance coming from, could it be from the "Divine Godness" from the cosmic unity or universal intelligence which governs us all?

Otto Loewi (1873-1961), a German born physiologist, won the Nobel Prize for medicine in 1936 for his work on the chemical transmission of nerve impulses. The initial idea that chemical transmissions rather than electrical transmissions were the source of nerve impulses was conceived some seventeen years before he had a dream revealing the methodology which he needed to prove the hypothesis. The rather simple experiment resulted in proof that his theory was right and as a result he won the Nobel Prize. Here we have the example of a dream which produced a solution to a problem which Otto Loewi had been contemplating for years. You may say that this dream was not prescient but the result of processes within the unconscious which had been working on the problem for years and once the solution was reached subconsciously it was delivered to him in a dream. If we accept this premise it still does not change the fact that the information arose from his unconscious and was communicated to him by his dreams. It involved information which he did not consciously have and the formulation of a plan which could lead to the Nobel Prize. It relayed information about matters in the future and if Dr. Loewi had failed to follow the solution as provided in the dream someone else would have taken home that prize that year. Once again we have some indication that the individual has some control over whether or not a particular "fate" is arrived at or not.

Srinivasa Ramanujan (1887-1920) was one of India's greatest mathematical geniuses. He reported that during his lifetime a Hindu Goddess would appear to him with mathematical formulae which he would write down. He claimed these dreams occurred to him throughout his life and they were a source of inspiration for his work. A similar dream to Dr. Loewi in that it provided scientific information to the dreamer which he had previously been unaware of and which furthered their careers. A helping hand from the unconscious which communicated to the conscious mind through dreams and which not only foretold the future but determined the future. In both cases, however, the dreamer had to be a willing participant in the plan. Any sign of egoism or failure to surrender to the "commands" of the dream would have doomed the success which each man found in his dream world.

Then there was the story of nine year old Derek Blankenship whose dream that his house was on fire was so real that it woke him up. His family was still asleep in those early morning hours when he smelled the smoke after awakening from his dream. He realized his home was on fire and he woke everyone and got them out of the house in time to save their lives. This came from a storey published By Allie Robinson June 07, 2011 in Bristol, Tennessee.

Finally we have this series of dreams of a woman being warned by her unconscious of a serious medical condition which she was not aware. She had the following to say from a excerpt of her article;

THE LIFE SAVING QUALITIES
OF DREAMS

General Event with MARIE EBEL

"Dreams have been a very important component of my work as a psychologist. Also in my own life dreams have played a major role. Dreams have been my advisers, they warned me of dangerous situations that I would have to face. They helped me when I had to make important decisions that were very difficult for me."

"In 1993 I had a whole series of dreams that warned me of the severity of my disease at that time. I was not able to realize it by myself although I felt unhealthy. My dreams became more and more intense and forceful; later their message even became specific much more so than usual in dreams. My dreams told me that I had cancer and that it already was in a very alarming phase. There were other dreams that showed me my death and my burial in all details."

This dream is more closely associated with President Lincoln's dream. Both of them had dreams which foretold their deaths. The difference is in the action which each of them took upon learning of their impending death. One took action which prevented the particular version of fate which was displayed in her dream and the other failed to take sufficient action necessary to avoid that same fate. It is also interesting that both of them had a series of dreams which they reported as did our mathematician. I cannot with a clear mind come to a conclusion which is anything but the fact that some dreams are early warning systems which if listened to and attended to can change the course of one's destiny. It is clear that both Lincoln and Ms. Ebel would both have died if they had both failed to attend to the warnings provided to them. Ms. Ebel did have the benefit of multiple dreams with an ever increasing urgency which finally created some necessity to take action. President Lincoln only reports one dream about his death, perhaps he needed recurring warnings to avoid his assassination, to believe in the efficacy of his nocturnal visions.

Looking at these examples from a purely evidentiary perspective we have credible witnesses relating events which occurred to them personally, not related to them by someone else (hearsay). This is a good witness for any case you might want to make. There is no reason to doubt the telling of the story of the dream therefore the only doubt that can arise in association with the nature of the dream and reality is our own interpretation of what it meant. Objectively it is clear that the dreams themselves depicted events to occur in the future or future discoveries which were foretold in the dreams. None of the dreamers had any motive to lie about the dreams in fact it diminishes their own role in the discovery if they tell us that they received their solutions from somewhere other than their conscious minds. Without the dream they were still floundering. Relating the fact that they made such significant discoveries through their dream life also has to cast some serious doubts as to their scientific and rational mindset and as such they would have advanced their own credibility further by not relating the dream.

Now we are faced with the only alternative which we have which is to discredit such testimony by interpreting the facts in a way which diminishes the reality as testified to. The rationalist, that person who believes only in what she can smell, taste, touch and put in the bank would make the argument that all the dreams arose from sensory perceptions which the dreamer may not have consciously registered at the time but which none the less registered in their consciousness. Lincoln certainly knew that he was a prospective target of assassination during the Civil War. Ms. Ebel even reported that she knew something was physically wrong with her though she wasn't exactly sure what it was. Her body knew the problem and she was consciously aware of the difference in her body from a healthy state. As a result of that although she may not have consciously put the facts together immediately as her health deteriorated her consciousness became more focused on the condition. So the rationalist would say both of these dreams were merely contents of consciousness (not unconsciousness) finally receiving the attention which they deserved and while the mind was at rest (in a dream state) it was able to rise to a level where sufficient attention was paid to it for it to become operationally conscious.

That particular argument may raise some doubts with a jury or judge but in the wider context of dreams of Siddhartha's mother which were formulated before his birth and foretold of his destiny the same logic will not hold up. In that case they would have to assert that the dream of his mother set in motion a pattern of thought among family and the other royal household that this child would be very special and had a "destiny" which must be fulfilled. As a result they all either consciously or unconsciously moved the child towards that destiny. It had nothing to do with a supernatural power that preordained the fate of this child but merely a progression of rational behavior set in motion by a "wish" of greatness for her child by the mother. Isn't that the same thing though, fate doesn't necessarily have a set game plan it only has a fixed goal. It is interesting to see in a courtroom or in any setting where arguments over factual occurrences take place what a diverse characterization of the event or events can materialize depending on the perspective of the parties involved. What you perceive is determined by who you are and what you believe.

I remember a case once against a dentist who had done some work on my client. My client had gone to a doctor for problems he was having with his respiratory system and while the doctor was reviewing the x-ray of his lungs he turned to my client and asked him when he last saw his dentist. My client thought it to be a very peculiar question from his physician who was treating his pulmonary problems but gave him the information without any question. The physician then showed my client the x-ray which clearly displayed a dentist drill bit lodged in his lung. During the deposition of the dentist he was asked why he didn't inform the patient of the lost drill bit. His response was that he knew he had lost it but the probabilities were very slight that it would have fallen in his lungs but more likely than not it went to his stomach and would eventually be evacuated. He said this all with a very straight face and confidence in his decision to not tell the man. Of course the patient was extremely upset when he found out that the dentist had to know but failed to tell him. The dentist was mystified why the patient was so upset because the problems he had with his lungs was not caused by the drill bit but by his pre-existing COPD and besides he never would have discovered its existence in his lung without the x-ray. At trial the dentist defended his decision. My client passed away before the trial and was not there to testify on his own behalf. His death was not caused by the drill bit and therefore the dentist felt more justified than ever. The drill bit did however have a very subtle and destructive effect on my client's mental health despite the lack of a direct causal link to his physical health.

The point is that we have a marvelous capacity to rationalize any action which we take regardless of its negative consequences to another and make ourselves free of blame. This too is a survival mechanism, at least survival for the perpetrator perhaps not the victim. Our ability to rationalize even the most horrendous behavior serves to keep us mentally balanced and maintain our "selves" as righteous citizens of the world. When we think about our ability to rationalize we must also think about our definition of evil and those characters from the past that have made the top of the "most evil" list. All of those figures justified their horrific behaviors, justified the slaughter and torture of untold thousands. They felt justified in their actions against humanity. Does this make us think of the supreme perpetrator of evil himself? It certainly feels like the dark prince has his hand in this sort of thinking, this twisted but effective camouflage of words which always leaves the perpetrator free of any guilt and in some cases feeling not only justified but "righteous" in his actions. What kind of contorted perspective does it take to convince yourself of your own righteousness when you are cooking children in a frying pan while their parents watch? Lucifer is the king of deception, the master of rhetoric, the muse of rationalization. He knows us better than we know ourselves and above all else he knows how much we desire to be "right" to be "justified" in our actions. He knows that even the most depraved of our species needs a sense of balance, a sense of "righteousness" and he provides it. He has made us the grand purveyors of self-effectuating grandiosity.

Satan thrives in the world of our fantasies not the reality. He breathes life into our blasphemies while annihilating any scent of the truth which stares us in the face. He fools us, courts us, tempts us, and finally captures our souls swallowing them with a contemptuous belch at their lack of substance, their tastelessness. If only he could get a hold of a vital soul, a soul of the light, a soul which knows the power of love, how sweet that would taste, how filling that would be, how satisfying. Those souls are beyond his reach although he never stops trying for he is if nothing else relentless. He knows that we are slaves to our sins, our temptations if we fail to seek a higher power to free us.

This entire discussion on fate, destiny, predestination in dreams, and our ability to change one's fate/destiny is in reality a way of defining whether or not there is a place in all of this for God. Do these ideas draw us any closer to the notion that there is a higher power operating in our universe which determines what our path will be? Without considering what that "power" may look like or feel like it is apparent that it does exist. The convoluted self-serving rationalizations which force the "dream" into an all too small box are empty of truth. They do not speak to the soul of the event but only to the surface. They have no feeling, no power and no stamina to endure intense probing by our consciousness, all of our consciousness not just the rational part. The dreams themselves ask for no clarification. They produce scientific formulas, mathematical equations, accurate prognostications, hit songs, warnings of impending death and other mysterious apparitions which arise from the uncharted reaches of our mind and beyond. Their proof is in the pudding. Their proof is not in a jumble of words which say nothing substantive in a very persuasive way. You can take that dream to the bank if you are paying attention to what it tells you. Because this evidence points to the fact that there is some operating principle which has the power to govern and determine our lives, it is evidence of a higher power, of a God. We will, however, before we end part one of this book, discover further proof of God's existence and the world lying beyond the curtain of death.

First, however, we will visit another in a series of instructive dreams which I had during the inceptive period of my religious revitalization and renewal. I was one of those who dismissed as religious hype the concept of being "born again". First of all it has a kind of "cheesy" feel to it. I considered it not any more than a catchy slogan to bring in the poor and miserable, to make them feel they have a second chance because the first one they got sucked. But I was wrong and my error could be found in my arrogance, my assurance of my own invulnerability in the face of adversity for the Dark Prince had had his way with me for a very long time. Once that attitude found its rightful place in the trash I was able to appreciate that being "born" into another mindset was indeed the description of a real life transformation which was possible and desirable. God does indeed work in mysterious ways. Seek him as you would seek your last gasp of air as you drown and you will surely find him. He is our last refuge.

WALKING IN HIS FOOTSTEPS

I stood on the edge of a jungle. Gathered around me were a small group of people, all of whom were emerging from the canopy of foliage to the edge of a clearing. We looked like a group of explorers, finding our way through un-charted territory. We were seeking a direction and we faced towards the swath of clearing that stretched into the distance before us. It was a bright day and my dream perspective put me above the group so that I could see my position at the edge of the jungle growth and the clearing before me as I stood there. I noticed looking down on this scene that there were elongated depressions in the clearing leading away from the jungle. They formed a pattern of sorts which dotted the path as it disappeared into the distance. Upon further study of the patterns of crater-like formations it became apparent that they were giant footprints proceeding into the unknown. My best estimate of the size of each footprint was perhaps thirty yards long. It was also obvious that they were impressions which resembled those of a man. From my position on the jungle's edge I came to a conscious decision that these prints marked our path, our way out of the jungle. The dream ended with that thought.

I couldn't help but recall that one of the very first in this series of spiritual dreams was of footprints following me, God's footprints. Now I encountered ones which I was following, again God's footprints, but this time larger more defined and leading me in a direction not following my direction. It was clear that my orientation to God had changed since that first dream I had months before. Was it possible that all that contemplation, that conversation with God (praying) had actually transformed my relationship with him and with me? After all that was what the spiritual books espoused that conversing with God, recognizing his possible existence and acting on it was a formula for self transformation. Of course if we have come to the point where we are in fact conversing with God, then we are seeking a transformation of our lives. People who are satisfied with their lives, content, happy for the moment anyway, do not aggressively pursue a "power beyond themselves" to fix their problems, their unhappiness, because they do not perceive that they have any. Even though the time of extreme anguish in my life was not a place I want to return to I have learned its central importance to my travel on the path which I am presently traversing. I would not change one thing, not one moment of pain or distress because in passing through that jungle of fear I found a clearing which led me to follow the footsteps of God. I am not talking about being a God I am talking about wanting him to lead me to a spiritual place, to the paradise of my own soul, where I can live a life which is nourishing, satisfying, free of anxiety, uplifting and beneficial.

I have learned that striving to be a perfect tool in God's hands is a far greater calling than being a perfect fool in my own. Since that dream I have strived to follow a path that the "universal being of power and light" could condone, that he could appreciate as being for him. I have never regretted that decision and it is perhaps the most important directional change I have or ever will make in my life. I am probably for the first time in my life verging on a state of "peace and contentment" without the necessity of material "pacifiers" to get me there or at least some pretence of there. Just writing these pages makes me so happy.

DEATH IS THE PORTAL TO
THE AFTERLIFE

I have had a life of coincidences and lucky breaks. I have always known this but have never considered where or how it arose; I just know that I have always drawn either people, events, books or all three to me when I most needed it. A good example is the subject of this section. Near Death Experiences (NDE) as I will refer to them are the next logical step in our exploration of the existence of God or something similar to God, that possesses his power but perhaps not his personality.

The story of how I came into contact with the book I felt was particularly helpful in exploring this phenomenon is insightful. I had a friend who had been suggesting that I read a certain book for perhaps five years. That book was "Closer to the Light" Learning from the near-death experiences of children. The book was written by Melvin Morse M.D. She had in fact given me three copies of the book over a period of the years I had known her. She would always ask me if I had read the book and I would mumble something about how I had started reading it but could no longer find the copy I had been given by her last time I saw her. She wasn't upset exactly but more frustrated with my persistent disassociation with her entreaty to me that I really needed to read this book. Well just shortly before getting to this part of this book I saw her again after a long absence and she had brought me another copy of the same book. I had been, as I often do, contemplating the next direction that I would go with this writing and I had as I became accustomed to doing asked God for guidance and inspiration. I knew when she handed the book to me that she had in fact given me the answer to my question of where to next, where am I going with this, what does it mean. I knew that my request for inspiration from a higher power had been answered. I also realized that it is very difficult for a person to discover something, even something very important if they are not ready to do the discovering.

I was finally ready to learn about the journey after death and this copy of the book I did not lose and it served as an inspiration just when it was needed not sooner and not later. I still recall that she would always preface her praise of the book by saying that it involved the experience of children who had died and been revived and how they did not have preconceived ideas of a life after death. She had an analytical mind and knew instinctively that this character of the book caused it to have more credibility than adults having the same experience.

Although the book was important to me as an introduction I am not going to spend an inordinate amount of time on the book itself but I will on the idea, the experience and what it means in the context of our exploration of the existence of some power we can call God and our existence after death.

A NDE is an experience which is common among people who have died and been revived. It involves dying and passing through a tunnel which usually ends in a light and seeing relatives who have passed away. It can also involve meetings with God and "double jumping" in heaven. One of the more curious characteristics of these common experiences of having died and come back is that many people reported having been given a choice to return to the material plane or to stay in the afterlife. Many of the children chose to return to their parents who the children knew were suffering terribly without them. Those who experienced NDE's always seem to consider them life altering experiences, happenings which forever would give then a new perspective on life and death which improved their second chance at life.

In my mind, looking at the stories of a variety of people having almost identical types of experiences in relation to their own near death episodes means something. The old saying, "where there is smoke there is fire" comes to mind when I think about these mystical occurrences. Of course you can ignore them and rationally pass them off as aberrations but that is just that little devil, rationalization, fooling us again, lulling us into torpor, making us a slave to its addictive allure. You have to admit that rationalization has medicinal qualities. It calms our nerves, makes us feel better about ourselves, and gives us all a common basis for agreeing on what the universe is and is not. The only problem is that rationalization if not controlled and carefully monitored by the truth inevitably leads to jihad, inquisition, Nazi Youth, women and children killed by a "robot" bomb which knew not what it did, therefore no conscience equals less conscience equals more killing because it might just work next time if we could only build a bigger bomb. In the end we can always rationalize our behavior just to calm ourselves to make the universe right again. We can and do use the tool of rationalization to squeeze and contort every truth with which we disagree into an explanation of our own design.

I for one am not going to assume anything more or less than what was reported. So we have people reporting a consciousness after death, a reunion with relatives already deceased, visions of an afterlife, meeting angels and Gods and then being given the choice as to whether or not they want to go back for a while or just stay put in heaven. This is sufficient evidence for me to at least consider that there is another realm which surrounds us and which someday we will enter. That realm is on the other side of the "line of time". Our residual consciousness after death is interpreting this event, NDE, as it has been described despite the particular background or age of the person who is having the NDE. As we know from previous discussions our consciousness defines our reality not only during this life but it appears after this life when we have gone beyond the world of time.

We need just a note here on nature of evidence. Testimonial evidence is the most useful in trial sometimes because it not only personalizes the facts but the recitation can be subject to cross examination and in that process the truth or more often the lie is discovered. The credibility of witnesses is tested by their motivation, their lack of deviation from the original story and the manner in which they deliver their story. As my friend said, children although not always the most accurate at relating the truth are beacons of light shining on the truth of what they felt and saw.

PART TWO

THE LINE OF TIME

We all know what a line is and sometimes we know for sure when we have crossed that line and sometimes we do not know. Sometimes we have to be told. There are other times when we cross a line and then we come back. That is what death is, it is crossing a line. An NDE is an event when we cross the line and then come back again at least temporarily. The line which we cross is the line of time. On this side of the line is "time" as we know it, as we worship it. As we are its' indentured servants, we know it. It is our taskmaster, our measure of success or failure, our cancerous sore that we know will kill us one day. It gives us everything and then takes it away. It will not allow anything to stand still; it forces us forward in one gigantic wave of panic lest time should stop. When time does stop, we then find ourselves on the other side of the line. Those who have had NDE's have been to that place where there is no time, that other side.

There is a period through which our consciousness passes which is defined by time. That period is what we are all living now. We are all aware that this particular time is delimited by our birth and our death. We have no accessible knowledge of where we were (meaning our consciousness) before our birth and with the exception of NDE's, which are not technically death but as close as we can come, we have no knowledge of where we are after death. This is an undisputable truth which we all carry with us and which we are all aware of and act on consciously during our "time" on this planet. As a result we are all living with a defined number of minutes which we have to experience ourselves and our world before our consciousness exits into another world where the delimitations of time appear to not exist, where our individual consciousness is immortal. If we take the first piece of this model of the life of our consciousness, on this side of the line, with all the known quantities and qualities which we share, then how do we best use this time. What do we seek and what do we desire during these undefined number of minutes which are allotted to us and what is time anyway?

> *"People like us who believe in physics know*
> *that the distinction between the past, the present*
> *and the future is only a stubbornly persistent illusion"*
> *Albert Einstein*

WHAT IS TIME

I think it is appropriate to talk about the question of what time is before we talk about how we use it and what we seek from it. Einstein says above that time is an illusion. A survey of the internet gives some interesting thoughts about time. The one overriding thought is that no one seems to have been able to definitively define "time", however, there are some aspects of it which physicists at least agree on. There appears to be an emerging concept that time is only a means for measuring motion. Of course the earliest inspiration for time was the movement of the Sun, Moon and Stars across the skies. From the website "BLOG" I found the following helpful article on "What is Time".

Mc TAGGART ON THE ILLUSION OF TIME

John Ellis McTaggart(1908) and many other philosophers have proposed that the passage of time is an illusion **suggesting that only the present is real**. McTaggart is famous for his A, B and C series analysis of time. A brief review is as follows:

The earlier and later aspect of time is basically the same as the arrow of time. The birth of a person always comes before their death even as these events become part of the distant past. **This is a fixed relationship** so McTaggart asserts it must be more fundamental to time.

The past the present and the future aspect of time is constantly changing, future events are moving to the present and then into the past and then further back into the past. **This aspect deals with the feeling of flow of time**. This **constantly changing relationship is also essential to the description of time**. McTaggart **felt that time is unreal because distinction of past present and future (a**

changing relationship) is more essential to time then the fixed relationship of earlier and later.

McTaggart is making the point that time has at least two important aspects. One is the sequential nature of time or the "earlier and later aspect". This can be understood as our birth always preceding our death and our youth preceding our old age. The process is unidirectional and apparently cannot be reversed at least as our consciousness is able to perceive it

The arrow of time points to the future from the present which followed the past. This is a relationship based on orderly progression, one action always precedes another. You cannot go backwards. You can make an omelet from an egg but you cannot make an egg from an omelet. As he states above this is a fixed relationship and a basic characteristic of that concept which we call time.

The second aspect of time is the "past, present, and future" aspect of time. As he states this is the feeling of the flow of time as moving forward. We understand in our lives that we have memories of a past, but at this point in time that is all that they are "memories". The past does not exist in the present nor can we return to the past because it is stored in our brains. It has been recorded on the tape of our minds and has no independent reality aside from the reality which we assign to it. The future also does not exist now but unlike the past we can visit the future, in fact we are destined to visit the future every second we are alive, because the future is the next millisecond beyond the present. Again as with the past the future has no present basis in reality except for the value, the reality which we assign to it.

McTaggart makes the point that this aspect of time, our way of describing time which we consider the most important is in fact the least important because it is not a fixed relationship but a constantly changing one. While the arrow of time describes fixed non-changing relationships the "past, present, future" relationship is continually changing and implies that the only reality is the present moment which is instantaneous. It is gone before we know it. The moment which we call the present is that gust of wind which passes across our faces and is gone. It is that instant where the future becomes the present and the present becomes the past all within the blink of an eye. When we consider time this way we realize that the time which we know, which we are subjugated to each and every day of our lives, is in fact a necessary fiction which our minds have created. The fiction has been created in order to organize our lives, as an attempt to control the "constant change, the constant motion" which we all experience in this our material existence. The motion is what defines time; just as the first of our species to define time did so based on the motion of the Sun, Moon, and stars.

So if the past is merely a recollection of the present moment as it occurred and as it is recorded in our minds and the future exists only as a projection of the past, our memories, then in reality the only "real time" which we can become aware of is this instant. Looking to define time from the perspective of past, present, future is less satisfying keeping this in mind. The concept of cause precedes effect, the egg before the omelet, is more satisfying as it is a verifiable concept, one we see every day and know it to be true. In our world, on this side of time we go to sleep and then die, we do not die and then go to sleep.

Those people who have experienced NDE's have left our time and entered into a place where "time" if it exists does not have the fundamental characteristic of the arrow, of the time we know. There were reports from these children of being given the opportunity to return to their life and they did. Those who did not choose to return knowingly returned regardless. They turned an omelet into an egg, at least from our perspective. They died, went to an afterlife and then came back to the world of the living, on this side of the line. In many instances that experience of reversing the arrow of time caused them to be transformed as to the relationship to time here on the material plane. Their appreciation for life, for the time of life changed for the better. It became more spiritual, less material.

There appears to be, if we take these NDE's as real, to be a place, not within our time, but out of our time, across the line of time, from which we are observing the universe. That place of white lights and deceased relatives is not a place which measures or describes time as we do. We know that real death is the final act and in our world and life always precedes death it does not follow it. This is a place which we enter when we leave our bodies to travel at high speeds through dark tunnels to arrive at the land of white lights and peace. There is some indication that this is not the final destination although angels and even God were encountered there but it is a place where we still have the ability to reverse our direction and return to our bodies. The ones who have experienced these NDE's shared common experiences as described above.

From the Blog website we find the following quote. "There is an underlying process of motion and forces from which time emerges, however what we perceive as time is mostly an illusion." In relation to this we have the following from the same article. Time may just be common currency or unit of motion making the world easier to describe but having no independent existence. Measuring processes (of motion) with time is like using money rather than barter transactions. This again suggests that underlying mechanism of time is just one means of describing the nature of motion.

WHAT IS MOTION

S o if we accept the fact that time is in reality a currency, a unit by which we can better define and grasp motion then where there is no motion there would be no use of the concept of time. Remember however that the concept of time itself is fundamentally a means of describing at least one attribute of motion. Does this mean that in the world of light and goodness at the end of the tunnel there is no motion or is it something else which seems to reverse the fundamental character of time as we know it, the arrow of time?

If we look to Wikipedia to give us some indication of what motion "is not" we find the following. A body which does not move is said to be *at rest, motionless, immobile,* stationary or to have constant (time-invariant position). Perhaps the afterworld beyond this world where we go after our deaths is one that maintains a time-invariant position. The time-invariant environment appears to be one whose output is not determined by time. Another way of saying that might be that it is an environment which is not controlled by motion, the movement of objects by force. That would certainly fit with the notion that deceased individuals are encountered in this other world and angels and even God. It appears to be common sense that this would suggest that time is not the controlling factor in this world. Is this a world of immortality where time is unknown and irrelevant?

In order to illustrate how different this other world would be in relation to time the following fundamental character of time is that it is not a "block universe". The block universe is a universe where the past, present and future all exist at the same time. It suggests that all things past and all things future coexist with all things present. This appears to be a discarded concept among those who are current on these issues and as a result of that confidence they can declare that because there is no "block universe" there are no time travelers. A time traveler would have to move from the past which exists to the future which also exists or vice versa. The prevailing theory appears to be that because time is an illusion apart from the necessity of describing motion or change that there is no past or future to move from or to. The only question I would have at this point is how you explain a place visited by patients who have experienced NDE's that contradict this notion of "no time travelers". They have travelled into the future, their deaths and returned from their death or near death to be exact and come back to life. Although that may be somewhat of a stretch it appears to be what transpired.

I understand that despite the overwhelming evidence that these NDE's are real, the scientific community shies away from them because of the reasons we are exploring here. They cannot be explained by science focused on rational explanations for events which cannot be captured within our limits of rationality, our politically correct concepts of reality, of time. So we dismiss them with our rationalizations. They are bad dreams, concocted when on drugs, psychotic episodes but not real, not anything which we can explain with our tools of science and our minds bound by the predetermined boundaries of acceptable answers. This sounds a lot like the problem we have with accepting the God concept. There is plenty of evidence that there exists in our world a creative power which manifests itself on the material plane but which is not bound by the rules of the material plane. It is a force which is undetectable and undefined by our physicists, just as time is or consciousness, but which nevertheless infiltrates our souls and leads us to a renaissance of the spirit. It is a force with which we can communicate and receive a reply, be provided a solution.

Remember the mathematical formulas, the warnings of impending death avoided, they are the hints of a "Godness" which exists and is at our disposal. God is too old fashioned we say, but is he really. If he is what he claims to be he created everything and is part of everything. That suggests that he is part of everything lame as well as part of everything not lame, even cool or whatever other word is used to define the state of "coolness" these days. How does the concept of God relate to that of time and motion? Well let's see if we can at least think about it and come up with some similarities.

The concept that both past and present are only constructs of the mind feels right to a degree. Neither can be changed "in the present moment" because neither one exists in the present moment. You could argue that the future can and is determined by the present as it becomes the past because of the action we take in this present moment. If I were to make the choice to get drunk and then go drive my car I would be making some decisions in the present which could determine what happened to me in the future, or at least affect the probability of what might happen to me in the future. So although technically the future does not exist now we can by the actions which we take now and knowing the probable consequences of those actions determine the future. Perhaps we would not to a certain probability determine the future but we could to a high degree of probability what possible consequences we might suffer or enjoy as a result of our actions right now. This all sounds so self evident, however, we cannot always know how our present actions, no matter how well intended, will affect our lives in the future.

Just yesterday there was an auto accident. A driver had intentionally driven the wrong way on a highway and crashed at a high rate of speed into an oncoming car. The accident occurred about 2:30pm with dry roads, good conditions for driving and a beautiful day. The victim, the forty year old woman alone in her Chrysler, was killed. She was a single mom raising four children. The twenty six year old who was driving the SUV walked away from his car without any injuries. His car burst into flames. He told the police when they arrived that he had intentionally driven his car the wrong way. My wife saw the accident immediately after it happened and a passerby had stopped and reached in the victim's window to support her head with his hands. My wife reported that she appeared to be dead then as she passed the vehicle. You read those stories sometimes where you picture the person getting up as usual going off to a day at work and then at 2:30 they are gone forever leaving behind the rest of us to wonder when our time will come. There are some things which despite the best planning in the world are going to occur and will not be pleasant or welcome. No matter what we do in this present moment the future present moments will deliver surprises. We as a species have attempted to organize our worlds with space and time and rules after rules so that we can make the prediction of the future more tightly aligned with the action in the present. We accomplish this by projecting our memories of the past into the future, like the arrow of time we scout the surroundings for clues to A plus B equals C. We want guarantees because we fear the unknown hand in the dark which threatens to drag us into uncharted waters where we have no control. But like the illusion of time the illusion of control is also the greater part fiction than reality. Even though we do not have total control of our environment there are many things which we can control merely by being attentive to the present and not "falling asleep at the wheel."

What is interesting is that if the only moment which is subject to our manipulation, the present, is but an instant of time, then how do we capture that instant to make the most of our future. It seems reasonable that the "present" for all its fleeting character is the wellspring of our existence. It is that source from which everything which we have comes.

It is the beginning, the birth, the creator of the cosmos. The past is dead other than our memories about it. The future is not yet born, non-existent other than our dreams about its potential. I read somewhere that unless you are conscious of the present you will not have any memories of it and it will be as if it did not occur. The example is given of going to a concert and falling asleep. When you awake the concert is over but because you had no consciousness of it, for you it did not exist. The present moment does not become part of our past without first becoming part of our consciousness of the present.

Coincidentally the basic postulates of Quantum physics say similar things about our universe. What comes to my mind is that our consciousness is busy scrutinizing our world, from a standpoint of survival, looking for threats to our existence. The only reality which it has to scrutinize is the present moment that is the only moment which matters. The lion which was there yesterday cannot harm us today as we sit in the airport ready to depart our safari vacation. Even though we can conjure up images of the lion drowsily peering out from the shadowy canopy of leaves, the lion that gave us chills as we passed by in the open jeep yesterday can bring no harm to us today; he exists only as a thought. The young children of the village near the lion's lair do not have the same luxury we do as they must memorialize in their minds the places where the lions tend to dwell and act on that knowledge on a daily basis. Their survival depends on it just as ours depends on not frequenting high crime neighborhoods late at night alone. Both of these events may not be occurring now but they have a much higher probability of occurring and resulting in harm to you if you have not recorded these memories for later referencing. Our consciousness of this "moment" and the recordation of the events which transpired in that moment in our memories are powerful tools furthering our powers to survive hostile environments but they are not real they are only projected possibilities of future reality based on our past experience. Their probabilities must also be calculated and factored into the equation of whether action should be taken involving risks of harm or whether we do nothing.

WHAT DOES QUANTUM PHYSICS HAVE TO DO WITH IT

———— ❦ ————

> Furthermore, *it is meaningless to ascribe any properties or even existence to anything that has not been measured.* Neils Bohr, Physicist

Quantum physics stands for the proposition that subatomic particles such as electrons have the ability to act like waves, which can spread in an almost infinite number of directions and yet once they are observed they collapse into a particle. The key being the act of observation transforms the "wave of possibilities" which the electrons possess to travel in a myriad of directions into a point at which the electron actually exists, into a single particle. The act of observation is the act of consciousness becoming aware of the electron. An experiment was devised to demonstrate the nature of the quantum universe.

The classic experiment to demonstrate what quantum physics looks like is the cat in the box experiment. A cat is placed in a box with a Geiger counter, and a radioactive material, and a bottle of arsenic. The Geiger counter is turned on only long enough for it to have a fifty percent chance of detecting radioactive emissions from the radioactive source.

If the Geiger counter detects radioactivity then the arsenic bottle is broken and the cat dies. If it does not detect anything then the cat lives. Upon observation the wave has collapsed into the particle, the dead cat. To an outside observer, however, the cat is both dead and alive until the box is opened and it is observed. The point is that the observation changes the state of the cat. In actual experiments a beam of light was observed as either a wave or a particle depending on the measure taken.

I have experienced the affects of quantum physics at work in my dreams. The act of observing an object, let's say a dog, in my dreams can either transform it into a vicious dog or a lap dog. The transformation is complete and happens at the instant of observation. The transformation is also related to not only the pure act of observation but the thought component of the observer. The character of the measuring device determines the reality of what is being measured. It is like the power of positive thinking. You think positive thoughts and you create a positive transformation of whatever arises from the "present". You think negative thoughts and you create an unsatisfactory environment. Perhaps this is where God comes into the picture. Certainly the concept of God is positive, uplifting, loving, nourishing and all things positive. Is it possible that to focus on God and the positive which is associated with him we can actually dictate the nature of the "present" by using a measuring instrument (our consciousness) which has only positive characteristics. The hypothetical which is relevant concerning quantum physics is not only does the observer determine the character but the observer determines what reality is. The Copenhagen Interpretation of the tenets of Quantum Physics supports this interpretation. Neils Bohr had the following to say on the observer determining the character of the observed through the act of observation, focusing consciousness.

When no one is watching, the electron takes every possible route and therefore interferes with itself. However, when the electron is observed, it is forced to choose one path. Bohr called this the "collapse of the wave function".

what is reality The Copenhagen interpretation attempts to solve this problem by saying that reality is what is measured.

Is it possible that nature, as it occurs in the present, is subject to transformation according to who is observing it? I firmly believe this to be true. Forget the mathematical proofs the physics of it because I did read that in the realm of quantum physics the mathematicians make certain assumptions and in fact hedge their bets by "cheating on the math" just enough to make things work out. So if we were to also cheat on the math just a little by not requiring the scientific proof which the scientist seems to have a hard time finding then I think we create our destinies, our futures through our consciousness. Sounds crazy although if you examine your own life and you are honest about it I think you will start seeing a pattern of results that coincides pretty closely with where your thoughts were, your consciousness on a particular subject. Is that the same as karma? Is it the same as predestination? Did God give us the power to transform our lives into anything we want to make of them? I think we can all agree that every act which we take is preceded by a thought of that act, a conscious consideration of performing that act. The person who takes his own life does not do it without first planting the seed and nourishing it in the garden of her mind. The man who intentionally drove into oncoming traffic and killed the unsuspecting woman wrote the script for her death long before he starred in the play.

Very little of what we do is spontaneous. We think our lives into existence by becoming conscious of selected pathways. The electron which has an almost infinite number, but not really infinite, is only forced to choose a path when it is observed. Are our thoughts any different? We certainly entertain a variable collection of random streaming thoughts in any particular day. We know that we choose from those thoughts and by so choosing we determine our direction, our path, our karma, our reality. God gave us free will. The story is that Adam and Eve ate from the forbidden tree, the tree of knowledge. Because they chose to eat from that tree, their consciousness chose a path which collapsed all other potential paths into that one decision and because of that act man was lost according to some theologies. God certainly had the power to withhold free will from man but he chose not to do that. Instead he allows us to choose our own destinies and we can include a God in that destiny or we can choose to turn our backs on God and hack our ways through the jungle alone. The reality is that we can choose God and all that comes with that concept, we can measure him, we can become conscious of him and once that action is taken the wave collapses and we now have a particle called God.

We are all very skilled at rationalizing. We are all very clever at blaming someone else for our problems and where we find ourselves on the road of our lives. If it wasn't for that idiot judge I would have won that case. Well perhaps if I had learned to handle that judge, focused my consciousness on her needs not mine, rather than lash out with a cutting reply every time she made a ruling which was suspect I may have had a different result. Perhaps if Abraham Lincoln had paid more attention to his dream, focused his consciousness on its meaning, the reality of the warning it contained he would have left office in a vertical rather that a horizontal position. Perhaps if George W. Bush had not let his consciousness focus on the personal dislike and animosity between his father and Saddam Hussein we would never have invaded Iraq and a whole lot of young men and women who lost their lives or their minds over there fighting a war of personal spite would have been spared to raise the own families. We would most assuredly have had more money for our schools, our poor, our communities, our roads but for the act of one man's consciousness focusing on revenge, focusing on self-centered school yard bullying. We want to blame God but if quantum physics has any validity we might just have to blame ourselves for what we create in our lives. Of course we can also choose the positive.

"God does not play dice" Albert Einstein

Quantum physics has raised the specter of certain possibilities as it relates to the nature of reality. They are as follows:

1. Your consciousness affects the behavior of subatomic particles, 2. Particles move backwards as well as forwards in time and appears in all possible places at once, 3. The universe is splitting, every Planck-time (10 E-43 seconds) into billions of parallel universes, 4. The universe is interconnected with faster-than-light transfers of information

We have already talked about number one. The fact that consciousness affects the behavior of subatomic particles is momentous. The question is how far does that reach into the affairs of our everyday lives? Is there any reason to believe that a fundamental principle in the subatomic world, a world of which we are composed, has no application in large constellations of subatomic worlds? Nature is beautifully simple and elegant. Nature is inexplicably wise and thoughtful about its acts. It is not disjointed, disassociated, it is the organic infusion of wisdom and order into an otherwise fractured world. It is the presence of a "Godness" which gently and consciously watches over us waiting for us to be conscious of it. Waiting for us to answer the knocking at the door of our souls, to turn to the very source of the cosmos and with humility submit to its wisdom by shedding our personal wills which are always at odds with the universal will of the Godhead.

We have to ask ourselves, how has our aggressive self seeking turned out for us? We know what the answer is, just look around. There is so much unhappiness, distress, lack of trust and love, paranoia, fear, greed, injustice, and evil that we cannot be proud of what we have done. Does the internet heal our souls? Do private jets and cars that cost hundreds of thousands of dollars serve the greatest number of people or are they just baubles for the wealthy, insignias of privilege, of the fall of the Roman Empire. Don't misinterpret me, comfort is a good thing but greed is not, especially when it costs so many other people so much. Ambition is also a fine attribute and when used in a constructive way makes the world a better place for all of us. There are no hard and fast rules about the nobility of the poor and the degradation of the rich. There are realities reflecting a vast disparity in the quality of life between the great majority of people and a silent and small class controlling an inordinate amount of the resources, wealth which every one of us has a hand in creating hoarded by a handful of citizens to everyone's detriment. Money is meant to circulate among all of us. It is the lifeblood of the free market and to allow it to be hoarded by a few to the detriment of many is contraindicated in a healthy and vibrant economy.

Number two concerning the possibility that particles can move backward as well as forward in time, contrary to the arrow time concept, seems to be what happened in the NDE's. Moving from life to death and back again seems possible. Number three raises the possibilities that every time we "consciously measure" something we create a parallel universe is interesting but not particularly helpful in our discussion of God and besides it is unfathomable and unmanageable even from a conceptual perspective. Finally the proposition that the universe may be connected by faster than light communications abilities would seem probable. Aside from the physics of "faster than light" the universe which we live in is "one" continuous living and breathing and expanding being. Why wouldn't it be wired for instantaneous transmission of information? How else could it manage such a huge undertaking, besides it is one immeasurable phenomenon, an intricate product of celestial engineering, a passionate cauldron of life, a fire-breathing mother of creation? I just read in the paper today that scientists had measured an atomic particle moving at faster that the speed of light. They are not sure what to do about this other than doubt the authenticity of the measurements, for to accept the possibility would turn physics upside down and we cannot have that.

We find ourselves facing the real possibility that we are the creators of our own life paths and achievements. It is one thing to say this and concede that it may be possible but it is quite another thing to know it in your heart and act on it every day of your life. If the nature of our consciousness, whether it be tuned to spiritual or material things, determines the quality of our lives then we are technically in control. Our consciousness being the "measuring" instrument, the observer and the particular character of our consciousness transforms the almost infinite possibilities for our lives into reflections of itself. The easy example is when your mind becomes fixed on an idea, it can be either simple or complex, and when it does you begin to see manifestations of that idea in your life. You just bought a new car, a brand perhaps you never had before, and although you never noticed it before there now seems to be a lot more of these cars on the road than ever before. When your consciousness narrows its focus to particular objects it then finds those objects, screening out others, and delivers them to our door step. The first pangs of desire for a thing can be felt within. You can feel your body tensing, your mind drifting into compulsive territory, gearing up for the hunt, the actualization of whatever it is that has captured your imagination, your consciousness.

It starts as merely a tickle, an itch and slowly grows into an irrepressible force which grabs us like a riptide and takes us into the depths of your particular desire where you wallow for a time and then are thrown on shore again, drained until the next time, the next calling from your master desire. The event or outcome of our thoughts is decided by the energy we put into a particular pattern of thought. Any addict will tell you that the "itch" starts with an insignificant thought which then grows into thoughts of addictive behavior which lead to the behavior itself. It is controlling the beginning appearance of addictive thoughts. They must be smothered, they cannot be given life, they must be strangled before they gain strength and control us.

How much time do you think a drug addict spends thinking about drugs, how much time does a sex addict spend thinking about sex, a gambler about gambling and how much time do we spend thinking about how someone has wronged us, or how we can make more money? The answer to all those questions is most of our time. Whatever it is consuming our lives and turning us into the slaves of desire we are allowing that demon to enslave us, it is devouring us from the inside out. It threatens us, belittles us, cajoles and courts us until we give in. Resisting desires is a bitch. There are no two ways about it there is nothing easy here. Have you ever wrestled with your inner demons? Did you win or is it one battle at a time, day at a time, trench warfare situation? Is there ever a time when those demons can be exorcised, can be diminished so that they no longer have any power over us? There are those who say once we have realized with our whole being that all those compulsions arise from inside us and not from without then we rob them of their power over us because they arise within only with our assistance. We must not water or give sustenance to these mind cancers but must suffocate them deny them any nourishment and they will fade before your eyes.

ASK AND YE SHALL RECEIVE, Jesus

We have already had the discussion about man's ability to control his own thoughts. The Id, the Ego and the Superego are the competing forces within our minds which to a large degree determine how we act and what we choose from the world around us. If a woman chooses security over passion or love she will get what she has chosen. Her ultimate happiness depends on the compatibility of her choice with her true spirit, her soul. We all face that same choice in our lives and although we almost always obtain the desire of our consciousness we do not always obtain an abiding peace and joy in the life that we live. The man who chooses a career in engineering because that is what his father did and it is a stable and well paying profession must live with that choice. If his heart and his passion can find release in that profession then he will find peace. If his choice was based on factors not attuned to his spirit then he will always feel incomplete. He may have all the desired possessions which we are all so driven to obtain but his heart will daydream, it will wander into the ethereal world of pining spirits and pass its remaining days there. It would be productive to look at what we as a species thinks makes us happy which will in turn tell us what our consciousness is seeking in the environment and then creating but first a story.

A friend told me this story. She had married a man whom she did not love but who had provided a very comfortable life for her and her children. She lived a life which many would envy. The husband ran a very lucrative business and the family lived a life of luxury with all the amenities which we dream of. They lived in a beautiful home in a restricted neighborhood which was the envy of all who visited.

They drove luxury automobiles, wore designer clothes, and generally had the best of everything. The problem was the absence of love between her and her husband. She told me she would go to bed at night and her husband would be turned away from her on the other side of the expanse of bed. She would be turned facing the outside of the home where the waterfall which cascaded into the pool created a soothing background for her tortured thoughts. She would watch the way the lights from the pool flickered as the water moved to the force of the falls and her heart suffered. She knew that this was the world she had always dreamed of and through much effort and sacrifice she had obtained but she also knew that it was a world without love between her and her spouse. She would lie there night after night, year after year and tears would eventually roll down her face and moisten her pillow, dampen the silk of her sleeping gown. The thought which inevitably brought these tears to her eyes was always the same. She would look at the elegant pool and she would ask herself if the pool could ever hold her, hug her and love her. The answer was always a resounding no and that was when the tears fell. There are many people who find themselves in similar situations. They face circumstances in their lives which imprison them, which torture their spirits. They see no solution, for the problem was one that they created. It was something which they desired with their whole beings at one time and now that they have what they always wanted it is like a poison which they are forced to take every day and they see no end to the pain, the self created hell. There are many things in this life which we are led to believe are the source of happiness, however, sometimes we have been misled, lied to. It is time to find out what experience tells us makes us happy.

WHAT MAKES US HAPPY

> A person will be just about as happy as they
> make up their minds to be.
>
> Abraham Lincoln (1809-1865) Politician.
> President of the United States.

There are the obvious things like going to Disneyland, seeing a good movie, loving someone and being loved by someone, watching your children grow up, having a puppy or a kitten, kissing, swimming, laughing, talking to a friend, working in the garden, riding your motorcycle, camping, boating, cooking, reading a good book, looking at the stars, sitting on a warm beach and even working. The list of course could go on forever, but we are listing those things which are passing away faster than we can absorb every ounce of their pleasure, slipping between our fingers even as we try to hold on to them. The harder we try to contain them, to never let them go the faster they fly from our grasp. Do you feel them slipping away even while you are in the middle of that happiness? Do you think that the time is passing too fast, if I could just have another half hour things would be better, I would be happier. Our concept of happiness is a fleeting one. It does not persist for long after the experience which caused us to be happy has passed but we capture it in our memories anyway trying to squeeze every drop of blood out of our pleasure our happiness. That is our nature. We desire things which give us feelings of pleasure, of comfort and joy. We just always want more. We are not satisfied with the portion which seems to have been allotted to us. Is that because the social media brainwashes us with messages about a new product which is guaranteed to make us happier, more desirable, less depressed and more popular? We all know the message. Too fat, too old, too short, not enough hair, too much hair. The message creates doubt, self-consciousness, a need to be different, to be loved if we could only change this one thing about us.

Science has provided us with answers to all of these maladies of unhappiness. It is the pill and there is nothing which it will not make better, happier. Is there anything you can think of which there is not a pill advertised to cure these days? I even saw a new product for "dry mouth". Used to be you could just get a drink of water and cure dry mouth but that obviously did not make enough profit for some drug company so now we have a pill. I wonder if you have to take it with water.

Before we wander into the balmy waters of happiness I feel the need to relate a story to you, something that happened just the other day which speaks to this issue of happiness. I was at the basketball court, as has been my habit for many years on the weekends shooting baskets, hoping to get a game going. When I arrived there were only two young men there playing a game of "one on one". They were both athletic and their enthusiasm for the game and the competition, the desire to win was clear. They were not interested in playing with an old man, someone who would just slow them down. They wanted to exist in the world of youth, power and invincibility. They were a good match for each other and a young woman sat on a bench glued to their warrior spirits, cheering them on. On my end of the court I was just shooting around when a homeless man approached me.

Now I live in a medium sized town but it is close enough to larger metropolitan areas that it absorbs some of the flavor of city life while maintaining an aura of small town America. The particular park where I play is lower middle class, working class, blue collar as we use to refer to ourselves. It is also a park which has drawn over the years, in addition to a lot of really good basketball players, a variety of pimps, their girls, dope dealers and their customers and the homeless. The backdrop to the game has always been a slow parade of girls looking for guys who are looking for girls, dope dealers plying their wares, pimps gathered in a corner shooting craps and the homeless on the edge of it all. All of the above have at one time or another joined in the sometimes eccentric games which develop on those courts. This particular homeless gentleman approached me and asked if he could shoot around. At the time I had no reason to deny him and he proceeded to talk, half to himself and half to me, first about baseball, then the way the game had deteriorated and how he use to be a basketball player who could touch the rim. He claimed he could still jump up and touch the rim but I knew better and if he had entertained a lucid moment he would have too.

Much of what he said I could not understand but his easy manner and his obvious delight in being able to shoot baskets with someone whom he didn't know and wasn't homeless was endearing. He wore the usual wardrobe of the homeless, boots scuffed, tired and too big, layers of clothing topped by a heavy coat, oil stained and grimy, looking exactly like the kind of coat a homeless person would wear and no one else. I did hear at some point something about helping someone up. He seemed to be debating whether or not he should go help someone get up but decided to stay and shoot baskets. He said something about his girlfriend as he looked across the park.

My basketball acquaintance was of an unknown age. It is difficult to tell the age of homeless people because they often are hiding under layers of clothing and layers of hair, layers of dirt and after all we do not spend a lot of time looking at homeless people. We prefer to look away and move in the opposite direction as quickly as possible. I would guess that he was somewhere between 35 and 45 but I wouldn't bet any money on it. I was surprised to see that this guy actually could shoot the ball. He had a history that had not always been on the streets. He had spent some time in the gym shooting baskets. In those days he had been clean and healthy, probably had a girlfriend who came to his games. He had good form and a good eye. I think he may have been drinking. I don't think he was drunk but he was "limber" he moved with that disjointed grace which inebriation bestows upon the body while the mind is put on hold. I thought about his history later in the day wondering how he had arrived at that state of affairs. He used to be a player a good player. I could see the remnants of a really refined shooting style. He made a few difficult corner shots. I was impressed. He was happy and each time the ball went through the net he lit up. He knew I could see who he used to be, he could tell the way I watched him after he made some tricky shots. He liked the feel of that. Someone noticing him, seeing the shadow of the boy that people used to cheer who had been lost long ago in the storm of homelessness.

I finally noticed an elderly woman moving very slowly across the grass of the park, picking her steps very carefully, hunched over, her path destined for the basketball court. Her frailty stood out against the raw power and determination of the two young men on the other end of the court. They both gave me a puzzled look as I played with this outcast of society. They had driven to the court in a new Cadillac Escalade. They seemed like nice guys, enjoying their youth, living their dreams. The old woman was my basketball companion's girlfriend. She could have been his mother or so it appeared to the untrained eye. When she had reached the court he escorted her to a seat on the sidelines and caucused with her for some time, head to head as if they had some secret business to conduct. Something important which they didn't want anyone else to hear, not that anyone else was listening. After a while he rejoined me. I noticed that the two of them had spread out some money on the bench space between them. It looked like a crumpled dollar bill which they had attempted to flatten out, to smooth the wrinkles but the dollar bill had resisted many attempts to smooth its wrinkles as it worked its way down into the world of the homeless. Perhaps once, when it was more presentable, it had been left as part of a generous tip at a fancy restaurant. There were also some coins scattered around the dollar bill. It was their savings, their ticket to nirvana. I had heard the homeless man say something about his girlfriend falling off the wagon as she walked to the court. He whispered it almost, so that she wouldn't hear, wouldn't be offended by his disclosure of her personal affairs to strangers. The woman leaned on her cane and watched her boyfriend play. He was happy to be able to show her his shot. I watched the obvious concern which passed wordlessly between them. It was a concern for their mutual health, for food, for a place to lie down and take a nap. A safe place where a quick nap could be had safe from other homeless or just kids out for kicks, looking for someone helpless enough to torture with impunity. The look lasted only a second but I noticed it. They had each other's backs because they only had each other.

When I was leaving the woman said to me, "I hear you have a pretty good shot". I just smiled at her compliment. She didn't have to say that and it made me feel good because I knew it was true and she was just speaking the truth she had nothing else but the dollar and some change. I asked her how she was doing as I was leaving and she looked at me and said sincerely, "I am doing fine, just getting older, harder to get around." She had no complaints, she didn't ask for money. "I am doing fine" she said and she meant it. She had someone she loved and who loved her. She had a dollar and some change and she was on her way to getting something to drink but in that moment, homeless, old, abandoned by all but my ragged shooting companion, and barely able to walk on her own power across the park, she was just fine. She had accepted her circumstances and knew who she was. I would hazard to say for that moment I saw her she was happy and her boyfriend was happy. She had abandoned the dreams she had as a young woman and she focused on one day at a time, getting from one end of the park to the other on her own power. She looked to be eighty but my intuition told me she was probably in her mid fifties. The two young players on the opposite end of the court tried to ignore all three of us. They were confused by what was going on and it made them angry, uncomfortable. They felt the need to leave. The old woman and her boyfriend were not uncomfortable, were not angered by snubs and disparaging looks, they were past that stage. They held no false images of themselves, those had been abandoned a long time ago as being too time consuming, too difficult to maintain.

I thought later that what we have lost, are losing, all of us is compassion. It is perhaps one of our species greatest gifts and we are losing the ability to feel it and thus to practice it and as a result we all suffer. Is it because we have been hardened to by these difficult times to screen out anyone's misery but our own or those we love? It is really too much when you think about it to become emotionally involved, even for a short time with someone else's problems, their unhappiness. Those times when we are forced to view those less fortunate it upsets us and we become angry at them for not hiding their neediness more effectively. It is hard to live the dream when you have people standing around you whose dreams have shattered into a million shards of broken promises and forsaken hopes. Those young dreamers at the basketball court had to leave they couldn't stay, it was too uncomfortable, to stay too long would force them to consider a time when dreams may not come true and that was too painful.

> *Remember, happiness doesn't depend upon who*
> *you are or what you have, it depends solely upon*
> *what you think.*
> Dale Carnegie (1888-1955) American writer.

Once again I visited the world's largest library with a click of my mouse, looking for the answer to the question, "What makes us happy"? The answers were interesting and I list them below. From the "Joyful Days Website" we have the following.

JOYFUL DAYS WEBSITE

The one thing most studies on happiness agree on is this: **family** and **relationships** are the surest way to happiness.

Close behind are **meaningful work**, **positive thinking**, and the **ability to forgive**.

What does not seem to make people happy are money, material possessions, intelligence, education, age, gender or attractiveness.

In rough order of importance, here are the factors that make us happy and what you can do to increase happiness in your life.

1. FAMILY AND RELATIONSHIPS, 2. MEANINGFUL WORK, 3. POSITIVE THINKING, 4. GRATITUDE, 5. FORGIVENESS, 6. GIVING TO OTHERS, 7. RELIGION AND 8. PERSONAL FREEDOM.

FAMILY

Those of us who are fortunate to be in a functioning family where love is generously dispensed and graciously received are very lucky indeed. We know how comforting it is to be part of a larger group of people who we have grown up with, who we have shared our heartaches with and who cared. Family does not always have to be derivative of blood relationships but those relationships are always special just because there is a biological nexus which binds family members together. It is a bond that cannot be denied but which does not always lead to positive relationships. The key to this well of happiness is the sense of belonging and knowing from whence you have come. People who know your history have seen you fall and rise, love and hate, come and go and they always feel a part of you in them. Family is the bedrock, the foundation of our specie's ability to contain our wanton desires and express our noble virtues. Family makes us all strong when the family is built on trust, love and respect. Without a strong basis in the family we cannot contain the compulsions of the Id because family teaches us to always consider others and not only ourselves. When our thoughts contain others well being we are forced to modify our behavior to curb the self indulgent urges and compulsions which drive us, often times to total self-destruction. So family contains us and it contains us with love.

We all seek love, in all its forms only to discover that real love cannot be denied, cannot be feigned, it always rises above the imitations. Love is the most wonderful of all human emotions because it benefits everyone who is capable of knowing it and understanding it. It makes us sublimely happy when it strikes our hearts and we can never get enough of it and there is an infinite capacity for loving. Family is the crucible within which love can be bred and the center from which it can spread into the universe. A person who loves draws others to them without understanding why.

RELATIONSHIPS

R elationships are similar to family but without the genetic matrix. We all value our friendships and often times we love our friends. We look forward to talking to them, seeing them, and just knowing they are there. They, unlike family, are not predisposed to accept you, to like you, to endure your repetitive stories about yourself. They are special because they chose you and you chose them from all the people in the world you have come in contact with. That is special and that is something family does not have. We cannot choose our family and the only way we have friends is by choice, mutual consensual choice. Good friends make us happy. We enjoy their company and their honesty. They know us and as a result of knowing us they have chosen to be with us. That is a powerful agent for binding people together. Our real friends are the ones that we never let go of no matter how seldom we see them or hear from them. In that way they are like family because there is not an expiration date of friendship just like there is no expiration date on family. Families are forever. Friendships are forever. We are all made better happier, healthier, wiser and more fulfilled by our friends and family.

I am not of course saying that we do not have times with our friends and family when we are not happy. There are times when both of them make us quite unhappy, miserable. These times, however, if examined closely enough usually involve an act of selfishness which strains the bond, which erodes the trust. We can then choose to hold onto this distrust, this anger forever or we can forgive, let it go and move back into love from that place of anger and hurt which just creates more anger and hurt. Of course there are families which are dysfunctional and they do not contain love. I see broken families every day I go to the office. There are always reasons for families and relationships deteriorating and usually it can be traced to a slavish indulgence in personal gratification. Others are only used and when their utility is non-existent they are discarded, not always physically but psychologically. That is not love.

A RELATIONSHIP WITH GOD

I believe now, after many years of being immune to the idea that a relationship with a "God", of whatever stripe you might want, is crucial to our well being. It is an essential relationship for us to enter into, if we are capable, because it teaches us what love is and shows us what compassion feels like. It opens our hearts to all people and teaches us forgiveness and virtue. I know it sounds corny, lame, and just goofy but I can tell you from personal experience it is anything but those things. It is really indescribable as it should be. God as we have noticed is beyond description and in many ways incapable of being known fully. We are for the most part just too small, too insignificant in time and spirit to comprehend the vastness of all things which he represents. It is like trying to measure the speed of light with a stopwatch. But we can know him in part and have a relationship with him that is mysterious and incredible. I am not talking about a public relationship where you go to the bus station and stand on a box and shout "Praise the Lord". I am talking about a private relationship of your own making which you carry with you everywhere you go. You always use it as a guide in making decisions and it heals you. It cleanses you of those things which need cleansing and it lifts the burden of doubt and anxiety which we so dutifully carry though life with us. It is a relationship which is always at your service which never abandons you and never disappoints. It is however a relationship and relationships require attention and effort. Our relationship with God is no different. One of the great misconceptions is that a relationship with God is a one way street once we have acknowledged him. The belief is that the only act which we need to perform in this relationship is to accept God as real and pray to him occasionally and we are home free. It is no wonder that in these days people don't trust God because he fails to live up to our childish expectations of what he expects of us and we of him.

Being a child of God is not the same as acting like a child in your relationship with God. How many of your friends or family would tolerate that kind of a one way relationship? Very few would be the answer. Why would God tolerate that kind of a relationship? The fact is that a relationship with God is difficult to originate, cultivate, nourish and grow because it requires so much faith, blind faith. It will be the most difficult relationship which you have ever entered into. It requires strength, courage, surrender, humility, and self denial but it creates a life which is unexpected in its fullness, its purpose, its equipoise. To develop true faith and true belief requires a lifetime maximum sustained effort in searching for the connection to God and using it. Once the connection is made our burdens melt away as the snow on the mountain peaks in the summer. It is however a relationship which always has the potential to be greater than it is. A stronger belief, a deeper commitment to doing what is right, an abiding faith are all the products of keeping this relationship as a priority. In the process of the evolution of that relationship we are transforming ourselves in to better, nobler and higher forms of what we once were. Just like going to the gym or exercising on a regular basis transforms our bodies into a more perfect example of what it is meant to be so does our daily attention to our place in the spiritual world transform our souls into a more perfect example of what the ruler of the cosmos intended us to be. It requires a effort beyond going to church every Sunday. It requires putting your goal of spiritual growth in the center of your life. It requires striving for perfection.

There is one other thing about a relationship with God that makes it a necessity to attain a level on the evolutionary scale which rises above our animal roots. A relationship with "God", a power greater than we are, is indispensable to achieving our maximum potential here on earth. Just a minute you might be saying that is quite a stretch. Actually it is not a stretch at all it is just a statement of fact. We all know that our lives and our goals for ourselves are circumscribed by our thoughts. Our thoughts are products of our environment, our family upbringing, our religion or lack of religion, and our experiences in our lives which have left an indelible footprint on our personality and which limit us. We are all a well constructed bundle of thoughts which create invisible barriers which our minds and our thoughts refuse to let us go beyond. We are prisoners of our ideas about ourselves and the world around us. As prisoners we are confined within our self made cells of ideas which are more effective than iron bars in imprisoning our selves our potential selves.

I see this all the time in my clients both male and female. They are caught in a marriage that they no longer want to be a part of or their spouse no longer wants to have a part of and they describe what their lives have been like. It is difficult to believe that in 2011 after decades of women's rights movements and education about domestic violence that women and men still accept it as somehow an undeniable part of what a relationship is. I am always amazed by both women and men who remain in relationships where they are abused either physically or emotionally. The emotional abuse which is more commonly spoken of is the most destructive to the mind, the self concept. A physical wound can heal but the constant message received from a spouse everyday that you are fat, ugly, stupid withers the soul, it dismantles any sense of self worth. The point here is that women and men suffer the gravest insults from their partners. They are cursed at by their spouses and children, they are spat on in public, they are humiliated in front of friends and they are generally made to feel like they are worthless.

The surprise is that they accept these insults and degradations; they accept the accusations as at least partially true because they have a mental construct which allows that insult to be true somewhere in their minds. If the insult does not find fertile ground to grow within the context of our own thoughts about us then we will not stay in or allow that behavior from a spouse. If it is contained within our own thoughts as a possibility then we will remain. The prison of our thoughts defines our life. A similar example is the man or woman who dreams of great things but who thinks in their hearts that they are incapable of attaining those dreams. Our cell secures our escape from our limited version of ourselves and without help we cannot pass beyond the bars of our thoughts about ourselves.

The only possibility of escape from our own limitations which we place on ourselves is to relinquish our positions, redefine the boundaries of the prison which we inhabit. We cannot, however, accomplish that without relinquishing our will, our mental construct which controls our every move to a greater power. Do you ever wonder why you see so many athletes, movie stars and generally successful people thanking God for their success? Do you think that is just a coincidence, a publicity stunt or is it possible that those people who all accomplished something which they considered at one time in their lives as being beyond them actually received help from God? We come to describe ourselves as an individual with distinct limitations. God on the other hand defines us as individuals without limitations. Because of his perspective he knows what we are capable of if he is allowed to take charge. He has fashioned you, groomed you, nurtured you and instructed you through the events of your life to excel. He also understands that most of us do not have a sufficient belief in ourselves to rise to our greatest heights without letting go and allowing him to take charge. We must relinquish the keys to the jail cell and allow God to unlock it, because we are incapable of doing it ourselves, so that he can help us soar.

I remember the night before my mother's funeral I had a dream about her. She appeared in my dream as she looked as a young woman and without saying anything to me I could see that the heavy burden of life which she carried with her always was gone. She smiled because her spirit had been let free to soar and you could see it in her face, her demeanor. She was liberated from the internment camp of life and she was happy. I could never remember her being very happy for very long. She had a hard life with many difficult times which slowed her step, dampened her heart and bowed her head. She was not that woman in my dream. She was free and she was happy. A relationship with God is a blessing which no one should miss. The question is whether that particular relationship, an intimate one based on surrender, can originate anyplace other than a place of desolation of the spirit. Without a doubt it is clear that it cannot originate without surrender to the will of the universe the cosmic law which governs all that we see and experience. We are not in charge and we never will be despite our futile attempts to convince ourselves and others that we are. We know in the quiet of the night when no one else is observing and our minds are taking a break from the incessant posturing which is required to successfully navigate the days' events that we do not make the rules. We know if we can only pull back the curtain of our intellectual and cultural arrogance long enough to see what is on the other side, the scary side of the unknown, that we are only minutia in the flow of life. Our nobility, however, our relationship to that cosmic deity makes us all holy, makes us all eternal and an integral part of the universal brilliance which rules us all. When we realize that then we no longer have to "cheat on the math" because in that place there is no need to cheat everything is exactly where it belongs, doing what it is meant to do.

I was watching an old HBO series the other day about the ruling class in England under Henry VIII called the TUDORS and there was a line in that show speaking about what it was like to be living at the court of the King that went something like this. "Living at the King's court and being exposed to him every day is like living with the Sun, your life is full and bright but living out of the court away from the King is like living in a place of perpetual darkness." I was thinking how the sentiment expressed here is so similar to what it is like to live outside of the knowledge of a God, outside of the grace of God for certainly to live close to God is a life of perpetual light while to live outside of his light his court, his kingdom is to live in a state of perpetual darkness whether we are aware of the lack of light or not does not matter. Sometimes you do not know the darkness you live in until you have been exposed to the light.

FORGIVENESS

This is certain, that a man that studieth
revenge keeps his wounds green, which
otherwise would heal and do well.

Francis Bacon(1561–1626)
British statesman and philosopher

I am not sure how many people would agree that
forgiveness is something which increases our happiness. I
am sure, however, that you cannot know it does or not without
practicing it. Why is it that we love to hold on to those times
in our lives which made us so unhappy? Why do we imagine
that we can increase our well being our personal happiness
by revisiting our most painful memories? Haven't we learned
that recalling pain increases pain, stimulates its growth? You
must admit that there are times when we absolutely cannot
forgive or even consider forgiving some act against us by
another. We would rather be burned at the stake than give
one inch of room for the transgressor to escape our wrath our
enmity. It could have been a wrongful taking of property or
money, a cheating spouse, a thoughtless act which pierced our
egos. It could have been worse. Someone could have caused
an unnecessary death, the end to a friendship, or poisoned
the well of friendship with some senseless destructive act.
They are all different degrees of the same malady. They are all

capable of being forgiven but more often than not they are never forgiven. You cannot wash blood off your hands with more blood.

If we take the day that we discovered the wrong doing as the day which our fury for revenge began and count the number of days which we have nourished, cultivated, and fertilized our gardens of unforgiveness then we know the number of days which we have chosen to dwell in the house of the Devil, to marinate our hearts in the acid of hatred and enmity. We do keep our wounds green by not forgiving and we keep our hearts closed and suffocated. We let the beauty of each day become tainted with the poison of our self destructive animosity. This hatred is fueled by the memory of a long ago injury which is resuscitated each day by our need for revenge. The malicious act is long past, dead and it is only revived by our recollection. It no longer exists in the present except by our constant resurrection of it. Forgiveness is not for the transgressor it is for the victim. The transgressor continues to inflict his past damage each and every day through you, your insistence to hate and your desire to feel wronged only prolongs your original hurt, the bleeding of the first wound. This is not to say that we forget about the hurt that was visited upon us because in this world which we exist today that can only be a request for replication of the same. We must use the information which we gathered from that experience and utilize it in the future when dealing with that perpetrator and others to keep further such harm from being visited upon us. But this does not preclude forgiveness for they are two separate concepts.

We increase our wisdom in relation to what causes harm while refusing to decrease our wisdom as to what is best for our lives. Long standing, festering enmity towards another is only destructive not beneficial. We are in the devil's playground when we hang on to the negative, the hateful, the violence of unforgiveness and we do not cross over into the light into God's grace until we forgive. The act of forgiveness can often open the door to wisdom and peace of heart. It transforms the perpetrators sins into a blessing in our lives a key to further growth and enlightenment of our souls.

MEANINGFUL WORK

Chose a job you love, and you will never have to
work a day in your life.

> Confucius (BC 551–BC 479)
> Chinese philosopher

I had to give this one some thought before it jumped on
the bandwagon but after some contemplation it became
clear that work is indeed or can be a source of great happiness
in our lives. The critical adjective here is "meaningful". So
before we delve into this any further it would behoove us to
find out what the combination of those two words means.
Although we all know what works means to us as individuals
because if we are working what we do at work and how we
do it is key to our happiness. I just read an article saying that
ten percent of workers are totally dissatisfied with their jobs
and one third of those working are looking for another job.
Another interesting fact was that approximately twenty seven
percent of workers are on the job physically but mentally they
are somewhere else. They are not engaged with this activity
we call work which takes up so much of their lives, they
are elsewhere dreaming while life passes them by. This group
does not believe itself to be engaged in meaningful work
and perhaps does not believe in the existence of meaningful

work. We all know, however, that a lack of belief in something does not make it "non-existent" it only makes it unavailable to the non-believer.

work   (wûrk)

n.

1. Physical or mental effort or activity directed toward the production or accomplishment of something.

mean·ing·ful

full of meaning, significance, purpose, or value; purposeful; significant: a meaningful wink; a meaningful choice.

The combination of these two words describes an activity which in a perfect world would make each one of us supremely happy. A purposeful physical or mental effort directed toward the attainment of a significant, important or valuable goal. Breaking that down we have an activity which we have voluntarily chosen to expend our efforts on, whether they be physical or mental and which gives us a great satisfaction. It gives us great satisfaction because what we are doing has a value to us and therefore adds value to the world. It enhances us, it empowers us and our efforts enhance others if our work is meaningful. It makes us feel useful and significant. Forget about how important society says the work is the key to this "work happiness" is what the worker thinks. There are some who can do work which all might agree is mundane and boring but if the one performing that job is consciously focusing on executing his work in a

quality and thorough manner then he will be satisfied and
that satisfaction will spill over into the rest of his life. This is
the ideal state of affairs. There are some who live this dream
and there are others who do not. Work for most people is a
requirement for survival. It is likened to our distant ancestors
needing to hunt in order to survive. They went out each day
looking for food, clothing just as we do. The goal was the
same. Many jobs do not offer opportunities to direct your
powers towards meaningful goals. Although all work is noble
when done honestly, completely and without complaint it
is a blessing to the worker and the recipient of the workers
efforts. Most of us have had jobs which were just a paycheck.
The paycheck was necessary and therefore any discrimination
between various jobs was dysfunctional when the goal was
to have a job, any job. When the rent has to be paid then the
rent has to be paid. There are no two ways around the reality
of food, shelter, medical costs and other necessities of life.

We are forced to work for the greatest part of our lives.
If we do the math it is clear that between working an eight
hour day and sleeping eight hours at night we have consumed
fifty eight percent of our lives between the ages of 18 and 65
or approximately 27 years of that forty seven year span either
sleeping or working. That is a huge part of our lives and if we
are not happy with our jobs, our vocations, our careers then
the quality of our lives will be drastically reduced. So how do
we handle the problem of working at a job to feed the kids
and working at a job that feeds the soul? Is a compromise
possible because we all know if one is not then we will always

be forced to feed the kids? In these economic times feeding the kids, feeding ourselves, housing ourselves has become as difficult as it has ever been in the industrial age in the United States. Regardless of what we are told by politicians about the recession being over in 2009 anyone with a pulse and who does not depend on the economy getting better to be re-elected knows this is a lie. So times are extremely difficult with double digit unemployment and empty houses boarded up by the hundreds of thousands because greed sucked the "honesty" out of the business paradigm. One of the results is gross unemployment, workers being taken advantage of because of their fear of losing their jobs, and a greater challenge in obtaining "meaningful work". A challenge, however, is part of what meaningful work consists of. A challenge is what makes us stronger, better, smarter, wiser, and in the end happier when it is overcome. A challenge also drives us to God if we are so inclined, sometimes even if we are not so inclined, especially if the challenge is sufficiently scary. Some people say that if you are happy you have no need for God for it is only the unhappy, the beaten, those clinging desperately to the shreds of their lives who turn enthusiastically toward a higher power who promises help.

We all know the myth and the reality of the American Dream. We know that millions of people from around the world have the dream of coming to this country and making it rich. That is also the dream of those born in this country. We believe, because we have seen it happen, that through diligent effort wisely applied to one's chosen work we can all better our stations in life. What we question now, in this moment is not our ability to work hard and smart but in the existence of opportunities for work where we can work meaningfully, where we can just work. We are a country of hard workers who take pride in what we produce and the services which we offer. We are at our happiest when we are working a contributing to our communities. We are competitive, ingenious and creative. There is not a product that we cannot produce or a service which we cannot provide. We need the opportunities to both earn a paycheck and to feel as if what we do is purposeful and worthwhile. This makes us happy.

There are people in the workforce who I meet everyday who are enjoying their work and contributing their talents to the accomplishment of goals with value. They are people of all ages in all occupations and they are happy. I ran into a seventy two year old attorney the other day who at one time was a Judge and asked him about retiring. He looked at me with what must at one time have been his studied gaze of perplexity which he bestowed from the bench when a particularly obtuse question was delivered by a clueless lawyer. "I see my friends retiring around me and then before you know it they get sick and die. I can't see any reason to retire, I am enjoying my practice and I love what I am doing". He said it in a "matter of fact" manner. It made sense. If you are doing something which gives you joy, keeps you in the flow of life and gives you a platform to do valuable work then what is the purpose of retiring at any preordained age. The next week I met a ninety year old lawyer who still practiced and went to the office at least a few hours a day. In response to my question about his plans for retirement he just looked at me and said he would work until he couldn't work anymore and it was clear that that day would be a sad one for him. He found himself in his work, it defined him and it kept him alive, lively.

I have this crazy idea that any job can be made meaningful. Some jobs are inherently meaningful because of their nature. Other jobs are not but can be made to be by how they are accomplished, the attitude with which they are approached. A dishwasher who comes to work to a sink piled high with pots and pans which will take him all day to scrub and clean has the opportunity to make that labor into something which contains value and purpose. Even though when he leaves the kitchen in the evening with an empty sink and clean pots and clothes damp from the seepage of wash water through his apron, he is fulfilled. He feels tired but under all that weariness is a sense of a job well done, a pride, knowledge that he has attained something of value that day and every day he scrubs pots until he climbs the next step of the ladder towards his destiny. He will always remember the value the rewards he earned in that job, the value which was not obvious but was nonetheless there. The value may be to only him, to the rock hard determination and willpower it will mold which will be an invaluable asset as he moves up the food chain displacing those souls one by one whose characters were not molded with fire and hammer. As in many things, forgetting the self is the first step in overcoming, fear, anxiety, doubt, hesitation and turning them into courage, confidence and compassion all of which equally benefit the recipient as well as the benefactor. Meaningful work or work accomplished in a meaningful fashion are both equally advantageous to us and can make us equally happy. When we have the opportunity to do work which we love then we are blessed.

> Work is love made visible."
> —Kahil Gibran, The Prophet

THE PROMISE OF
POSITIVE THINKING

~~~

> A pessimist sees the difficulty in every
> opportunity; an optimist sees the opportunity in
> every difficulty Winston Churchill

Next on our list of things which make us happy is positive thinking. I must admit I have always been a huge fan of positive thinking. Mr. Churchill makes the point very succinctly. Your thoughts are either taking you on an upward journey or they are dragging you down. Is it any wonder that a person who persists in looking for the good in every occasion possesses a sunnier, happier disposition and life experience? On the flipside is it any wonder that a person who is always seeking the worst in every occurrence, the naysayer is the village grouch, the wet blanket, the self destructing Assassin of all of our dreams, our hopes, our opportunities, our chances at love is most often unhappy, miserable as his hands have been stained by the choice of the dye he used to color the fabric of his life.

I just could never see the logic to constantly entertaining thoughts which have no positive value to them. We have learned in prior chapters that we create our environment out of the fabric of our thoughts. We have the chance to weave the tapestry of our lives out of hope, joy, freedom and faith or we can weave it from the discarded remnants of broken dreams, broken hearts, and broken spirits. Rest assured that whatever material that we may choose to weave this tapestry it will be reflected in the finished product. The material will define the tapestry, it will be the thread that holds the life together giving it its outline its substance.

I know for sure that I have never accomplished anything that I was convinced that I could not accomplish. Conversely I have never failed to accomplish anything which I was sure, I was convinced that I could accomplish. The accomplishment starts in the thought. Of course the work must be performed before the goal can be reached. We as a society tend to forget that these days. The current thought seems to be that if we can just convince ourselves that we are capable of accomplishing some goal that is all we need. That of course would be nice for those not so inclined to put the effort into the achievement of the goal. It is the same simplified vision of our relationship with God that we embrace. All I need to do is to put on a humble face, ask God for help and I have done my part, the rest is up to God. A convenient thought but a silly, lazy and unrealistic concept is what we have bought into. Meaningful work must be combined with the abiding thought that it is not just possible but it is inevitable that success will be achieved.

What is positive thinking? It is an apparently simple concept in which the thinker is aware of this stream of thoughts and controls them so that negative thoughts are discarded and positive thoughts are retained. The simplicity of the concept quickly evaporates when the effort to recognize and be conscious of negative thoughts is attempted. Most of us have a very difficult time keeping track of our thoughts at any particular moment much less controlling them. Instead we think or more accurately we access a preexisting thought and act on that thought. It is much easier because thinking is difficult. Deep logical complex thinking is a rare occurrence these days. Discriminating thinking which takes into consideration all the relevant factors which are present and proceeds to analyze them individually as well as their relationship with each other. The beginning point of analytical objective thinking is not with preconceived ideas or dogmas, or other strait jackets of critical thinking which obstruct the flow of ideas. It must begin with a blank slate and let the facts fall where they may. There is an old saying that "if you know the man's creed you can anticipate his argument". The application of a frame of reference, steeped in dogma, to solve each new problem as it arises only recreates or procreates the dogma in the disguise of the solution to the question undertaken. When we begin with a body of knowledge which circumscribes our freedom of expansive thought we are only regurgitating what we have committed to memory. It is much easier than actual thinking but it always delivers the same answers regardless of what the problem is. It is more convenient because we do not have to be anxious about any new dilemma which presents itself to us because we always reference our ready store of answers and proceed to unthaw the frozen platitudes and serve them up as fresh fare.

Our popular culture's concept of thinking is just this. We have learned certain facts and have appropriated certain knowledge and we use that information as we would use a hoe in a garden. We chop out and weed out every new thought which does not coincide with some thought which already resides in our deep freeze of a mind. It seems pathetic really that as the "most intelligent of all species" we are doomed to blindly run off the cliff of reality with our brains in a perpetual coma and our recorded memories playing an endless loop of "hail to the self" as we plummet to our extinction. If you think about it you will know that this is a reasonable assessment of what we refer to as thinking. Our educational system has been condemned by many because it seeks only to train us to memorize and then regurgitate. In large part that is what it does. There are, however, courses which require critical thought. Math is one of them. Science and philosophy are others. I always appreciated math for its requirement of analytical thinking as a key to understanding it. The solving of equations can be play for the brain or a veritable workout for the thinking faculties. It makes them stronger, sharper and deeper. Sustained analytical thinking teaches patience, orderly thought, concentration and sharp distinctions. These traits of a thinking man are necessary if we mean to survive and thrive. We must know when to discard the frozen patterns of thought which cripple us. We must jump the barricades of bias, prejudice, fear, and hate to blossom as the most enlightened of all species on this planet. We must shake off the shackles of stale and faulty fixed patterns of thought and once and for all grab the reigns of our intelligence and direct it into the unknown without a map.

I knew a man once who was convinced that he held the answer to all of societies' problems. Although he did not use the word anarchist that is a word that most closely described him although it was not all that he was. When I first met him his first words to me were, "so you are a liar, I mean lawyer, Every time he met me after that he would always inject into our conversation this statement. Every time he delivered it he did so with a very satisfied look on his face which telegraphed his complete enchantment with his perceived brilliance. He would argue the law with me and cite code sections which when he "dared" me to research them never said what he purported that they said. When that message was delivered to him his response would always include the "liar" reference and in his mind that always gave him the winning argument. Now the reason I mention this gentleman is that he is much like we are. Despite any evidence to the contrary he always managed to massage the facts and torture the argument so that he prevailed again. Just as he became a talking puppet whose monologue always followed the same path and allowed no doubt to enter his mind that he was right so do we follow the same road. It is difficult to catch ourselves doing this but we must start otherwise our foolishness will be the death of us.

Positive thinking is not stale rhetoric, it is hope springing eternal. Death follows life and life follows death in a grand parade of hope and doubt. It is ours to choose which trail we will follow and by so choosing we then choose our destinies. There is no benefit to turning an opportunity into a difficulty when we can fundamentally change the destructive projectile of our lives and turn difficulties into opportunities. There are many people who discard positive thinking along with religion and a belief in a higher power. "They are sheer rubbish and need to be placed where all rubbish belongs in the garbage," they say. I am still not sure what it is about certain ideas that have stood the test of time, lifetimes and are still hailed by many as a balm for the storms of our lives and are still rejected by so many otherwise thoughtful people. Is it so difficult to believe that a positive thought will create a similar act? Likewise is it not logical to consider the effect of a negative thought being colored with the same brush as its birth mother? Positive thinking is nothing more than the focused effort of marshalling thoughts of success, attainment, happiness, fulfillment and harmony. We have learned in previous chapters that the thought creates the reality. Our minds are like heat seeking missiles. They are laser guided bombs which once set for a designated target will inevitably reach that target.

The reason that positive thinking is one of the factors which people most often say makes us happy is for the reason that happy and positive thoughts seek out happy and positive people and experiences while creating an attitude of abundance which in turn draws all things positive to it. Is that so surprising? We all know it isn't, just look around, think about your own life and the creations which you have materialized by engaging in positive thoughts and then think about the destruction which has followed prolonged and obsessive negative thinking about anything. It is a proximate causal relationship. The act of clapping your hands together will always be attended by the corresponding sound of clapping hands. The same is true of negative or positive thoughts. A negative thought creates the sound of negativity and the birth of negative circumstances while the positive thought creates its opposite. It is an easy enough experiment to try even on a simple matter. Be careful, however, that you do not destroy the positive manifestation of that experimental thought before it has a chance to fully bloom in your life. We all have this certain self destructive impulse which urges us to undermine our own progress, our own good. Perhaps we run from our near successes because we do not feel worthy or capable of actually living up to so much good fortune. It is a burden, we imagine, having such a bright light threatening to shine on you when you feel so unprepared, unworthy, even though it is the dream that you have held dearest in your heart for your entire conscious life.

Always think positive and create bounty, grace, joy and happiness in your life and in the lives of those around you. Watch your garden grow bursting with life nourishing acts whose seeds were positive thoughts planted gently and carefully in your mind and then cultivated with a steady and alert hand to guarantee their growth. We should rejoice everyday in our ability to create our lives through a steady and unwavering regimen of positive thoughts. The most positive thought of all is the thought of God. God encompasses all that is good, blessed, positive, and uplifting. Regular and steady thoughts on God create a field of love around the thinker which graces all who come into contact with that person. To think Godly thoughts is to live a Godly life. To recognize a God, any God is to acknowledge that there are higher powers in the universe which we have access to and when approached with humility can be helpful to us in our struggles.

GRATITUDE

"If the only prayer you said in your whole life
was, "thank you," that would suffice."

Meister Eckhart:

Many of us are neglectful of this virtue. It may be
because with gratitude we are always looking to
something which we already have, something which has
already occurred. It is difficult to see what we are holding in
our hand when the hand is always reaching from something
else. We can argue that most virtues contain a promise that by
their steady practice they can enhance our future prospects.
Prudence, justice, restraint, temperance, courage, kindness,
humility, charity are some of the virtues trumpeted by our
culture. All of them promise some future benefit if they
are practiced in the present. Gratitude does not make that
same promise and therefore it may be misunderstood and
underestimated.

The religious writers emphasize gratitude more than
others. Their gratitude emanates from the perspective of a
God who gives us all that we have and enjoy. They daily
remind themselves from whence their bounty flows. The
believers feel connected to the source of all of life. They
participate in the bounty of God and know it to be a
blessing. Those who do not share this perspective do not

feel as comfortable with gratitude. An obvious reason for that would be their lack of someone or something to be grateful to. God provides us with an obvious recipient of our gratitude and if gratitude truly makes us happy then true believers are truly happy. I discovered this for myself. A simple statement of gratitude, such as a thank you to someone or to God for help you have received from them is uplifting. To acknowledge that our lives are sustained by the grace of all those who give to us is to practice prudence. An abiding awareness and gratitude for the source of our own bounty, our blessings is a wellspring of joy in our lives. When we display or communicate our gratitude we are reminding ourselves of what it is that has come to us in the stream of life. We understand that it is all a gift.

When I was young there was a time when money was scarce and ingenuity was sometimes all you had to make dinner with. We lived in a small trailer behind a truck stop in Oklahoma. There were the four boys and my mother. My father was away as usual and our only source of income was the money that would sporadically arrive in the mail from him. When I think about gratitude I always remember the dinner we had one night in that little trailer. There was no money to go shopping and there were four hungry teenage boys looking to their mother for a means of filling their bellies. She solved that problem by finding a bag of potatoes and turning those potatoes into a heaping pile of French fries. I can still remember my brothers gathered around that table mesmerized by that big bowl of fries. After all these years that is one of the most memorable meals that I ever had. It not only quieted the rumble in our bellies but it brought us all closer together as hard times often do. Before we could eat those French fries we had to say grace. My mother insisted that we thank God for the food which he had brought to us. To this day I am still grateful for those fries and I can still see them sitting in the bowl in the middle of the table all alone. My mother knew how to make French fries of course now they would be verboten but then they were just delicious.

The list of things which we can be grateful for is always personal. There are people, jobs, money, food, shelter, love, comfort, happiness, health, relationships, spirituality, friendship, a warm bed, a cold beer, a crunchy apple. We just have to look around us. So many things right in front of us which we love and which make us happy but which we never show or express our gratitude for. An expression of gratitude is an expression of our knowledge that we are the recipients of a bounty which is part of the cosmic flow of "goodness" delivered to our doorstep. All we really need to say is "Thank You". Thank you my family for always being there and sharing your love. Thank you to my client's for coming to my door and trusting me to listen to you and assist you. Thank you to my cat for playing your silly games with me and making me laugh and forget my problems. I thank you God for making yourself available to all of us, just for the asking. Thank you for being there for all of us and for granting us an ever deepening peace the more intimately we get to know you. Thank you for calming our fears, keeping us from evil, for loving us and caring for us. Thank you for never abandoning us regardless of who we are or what we have done or not done. Thank you for answering our prayers and for giving us shelter from the evils that prevail upon us seeking to turn our souls from its affinity to the cosmic ruling force. Thank you for making me want to be perfect in your eyes.

I had a couple come into my office the other day. They were elderly, both leaning precariously on their canes. The man tall, now stooped over was quiet but his eyes were inquisitive. He searched the office for items that piqued his interest and he would ask a quiet question about each item and mull over the answer and search again. His wife took command of the situation by presenting her problem to me in a carefully worded summary which condemned no person but only cast doubt on their intentions with regard to her and her husband. It is not important what their business was but it was important how they conducted themselves. They told me that they had been married at 65 after the respective spouses had died. They also stated that they had started a new business at the age of 65, when they were still young they said. They finally told me they were both 95. They had obviously both led good lives and they were grateful for that fact. They were a charming couple who complimented each other just naturally each letting me know their respect and love for the other without saying those words. They were gracious, considerate and quite satisfied with their unpretentious circumstances. They exuded a sense of thankfulness for all

WILLIAM J. PARDUE

that they had now and in the past. I did not hear one negative thought expressed while they were in my office and my office is a breeding ground for negative thoughts. I admired them as they shuffled slowly out of my office moving like snows melting off the hillside, carefully, gracefully. They were grateful for long lives, loves, spouses, family, work, relationships, talents possessed, and each minute that they spent on this earth. They were content with their station in life after ninety five years of existence on this planet.

RELIGION

My religion consists of a humble admiration of
the illimitable superior spirit who reveals himself
in the slight details we are able to perceive with
our frail and feeble mind.

Albert Einstein

Just as a candle cannot burn without fire, men
cannot live without a spiritual life.

Buddha

Both of these individuals have been mentioned or quoted previously in this book. The Buddha if you will recall made the number one spot on the best individuals in the history of our species. Einstein is known to all of us for his groundbreaking discoveries in physics. Both of them have a special regard for religion, perhaps different versions of religions but still a "humble admiration of the "illimitable superior spirit" is shared by both of them and thus well put by A. E. I believe that all religions would concede that if there is any commonality among them that this phrase would be perhaps the reductionist's version of those shared traits. Religion after all is the formal and organized recognition of that "illimitable superior spirit". Beyond that simple organizing principle the religions of the world explode outward from the center in a countless number of pathways all of which lead the individual away from spirit which lies in the very center. When I say lead away I do not mean that in a negative way but only as a way of describing the place where we stand when we believe in a "spirit" a "God" which is the very center of belief where the essence of God can be experienced. Organized religions have by their nature a tendency to shore up their base, to establish themselves as the one and only or at least the most attractive religion. In doing this they must create man made rules and regulations which define their particular practices and beliefs and bolster those same beliefs through proscriptions of the faith. These rules may or may not reflect the true nature of the "illimitable superior spirit" but only the true nature of the man made vehicle which claims to know God's will and every rule associated with that will.

I am not denigrating any religion because at the end of the day man is a herd animal and he follows the leader. He operates more comfortably in a herd environment and when he sees the herd moving in one direction he puts his head down and follows the one in front of him. This is not a bad thing as it is obviously a trait which has taken us to the top of the food chain albeit we left a nasty mess along the way. It is also a trait which can be used both to man's detriment and to his elevation, spiritual and otherwise. Besides it is illogical and shortsighted to denigrate religions. We all know that there have been many religious persecutions which have been promulgated by the religious establishment itself. Religions indicate a universal spirit which we all recognize.

Their importance is in the revelation of and pointing towards this spiritual center.

The point is that man must be careful that a particular religion becomes more important than the "spiritual source" from which it originated. When instruments of man overshadow the spirit it is a sign of Satan's clever tendencies and his audacious frontal attacks while wearing the mask of the true believer or perhaps the reformer. The good thing about religions is that they bring untold millions of people into close proximity with the concept of God and his goodness. By doing this they are spreading the message that there is in fact a compassionate and loving "spirit" which existed before the churches, synagogues, or other houses of worship were even an idea which could be espoused to the hungry masses yearning for some greater power that could assist them in their time of need.

The question then becomes, in the context of happiness and religion, what relationships do they share with each other? Is there some proven benefit or detriment to holding a religious belief? Once again a search through the miracle of modern day technology brings the answers to these formidable questions to our fingertips within a matter of seconds. (Unless you have lived long enough that there was a time in your adult life when the internet was just a twinkle in some visionary's eye then you will never be able to appreciate the amazing resource that it is).

The research states without any prevarication that religious people are happier and healthier than non religious peoples. There is a long list of positive attributes and traits which are particularly characteristic of believers as opposed to non believers. I will list a few of the most striking examples.

Why Religion Matters Even More: The Impact of Religious Practice on Social Stability
By Patrick Fagan PhD *December 18, 2006*

In Dr. Fagan's article he leads with a litany of benefits enjoyed by religious peoples."

"Regular attendance at religious services is linked to healthy, stable family life, strong marriages, and well-behaved children. The practice of Religion also leads to a reduction in the incidence of domestic abuse, crime, substance abuse, and addiction. In addition, religious practice leads to an increase in physical and mental health, longevity, and education attainment. Moreover, these effects are intergenerational, as grandparents and parents pass on the benefits to the next generations."

You must admit that is quite a list. It is an impressive list because the question has to be asked why is it that religion has such a significant positive effect in so many areas of our lives. Other cites reflect the same information.

THE DAILY GALAXY/DOES RELIGION MAKE PEOPLE HAPPIER?

"Professor Andrew Clark, from the Paris School of Economics, and co-author Dr Orsolya Lelkes, from the European Centre for Social Welfare Policy and Research, analyzed the a variety of factors among Catholic and Protestant Christians and found that life satisfaction seems to be higher among the religious population. The authors concluded that religion in general, might act as a "buffer" that protects people from life's disappointments."

Again we have the fact that religious people have greater life satisfaction. He goes on to say.

" . . . . but our analysis suggested that religious people suffered less psychological harm from unemployment than the non-religious," noted Professor Clark. "They had higher levels of life satisfaction".

"Data from thousands of European households revealed higher levels of "life satisfaction" in believers. Professor Clark suspects that a variety of aspects are at play, and that perhaps a "religious upbringing" could be responsible for the effect, rather than any particular religious beliefs."

"The researchers say they found that the religious crowd tended to experience more "current day rewards", rather than storing them up for the future. Previous studies have also found strong correlations between religion and happiness."

Yet another scientific study corroborating the relationship between religious beliefs and the experience of more satisfaction out of life. A happier life is a scientifically proven result of holding religious beliefs. How do you argue with that proven relationship? Do you say the figures were skewed, the research was faulty and the conclusion illogical? We have learned in previous discussions that man has an infinite capacity to take any piece of information, any fact and turn it into an apparent falsehood. Perhaps one of the most destructive traits which mankind possesses is his ability to rationalize anything, any situation, any facts to suit his own predetermined beliefs. Is there any trait which is more destructive? It is certainly the leading cause of every atrocity which has ever visited the human race. You see it every day on the job, in the newspapers, discussions with friends, talk radio.

We all try so hard to always be right, to always have the right answer, to always know what is best for everyone else when we don't even know what is best for ourselves. We fear being wrong, admitting that we might be wrong above just about everything else. What is it about us that makes us so afraid of being vulnerable for that minute of admitting that we are wrong and actually learning something new, evolving into the next higher level of thought, of living? I have had as much difficulty as anyone when it comes to this concession of fault of being wrong. It is so difficult perhaps because we have put so much emphasis, so much effort in our version of ourselves that there is no room for improvement, there is only time and effort available for holding the fort, defending your position, buttressing your ego.

Let's get back to why religion makes us happy. "Professor Leslie Francis, from the University of Warwick believes that the benefit might involve the increased "purpose of life" experienced by many believers. He posits that it may not be as strongly felt among nonbelievers." "These findings are consistent with other studies which suggest that religion does have a positive effect. "Let's look at one last reference just to get a further sense of what all of these studies indicate and to impress upon us that these are not just random findings without meaning for all of us who care to think carefully about their conclusions.

What Religion Can Do for Your Health /BELIEF NET

Why practices like prayer and attending church can have a powerful effect on our mental and physical well-being.

BY: Interview by Lisa Schneider

"Dr. Harold G. Koenig is co-director of the Center for Spirituality, Theology, and Health at Duke University Medical Center, where he also serves on the faculty as Professor of Psychiatry and Behavioral Sciences, and Associate Professor of Medicine. Dr. Koenig is the author of many books, including "The Healing Power of Faith," "Faith and Mental Health," and "Spiritual Caregiving," and he has been nominated twice for the Templeton Prize for Progress in Religion. He spoke with us recently about why he believes being part of a religious community can make people healthier—and happier."

In Dr. Koenig's interview he has some interesting insights into how religion makes us happier. When asked about the health benefits of both prayer and religious practice he stated:

"Beyond the effects of prayer, do you believe religious practice can lead to other health benefits? What are they?

"Bear in mind that these benefits are not intended, they're kind of a consequence of going to church or praying or reading the Bible or being religiously committed. They're kind of a side effect of being religious for more valid, more intrinsic reasons."

"The benefits of devout religious practice, particularly involvement in a faith community and religious commitment, are that people cope better. In general, they cope with stress better, they experience greater well-being because they have more hope, they're more optimistic, they experience less depression, less anxiety, and they commit suicide less often. They don't drink alcohol as much, they don't use drugs as much, they don't smoke cigarettes as much, and they have healthier lifestyles. They have stronger immune systems, lower blood pressure, probably better cardiovascular functioning, and probably a healthier hormonal environment physiologically—particularly with respect to cortisol and adrenaline [stress hormones]. And they live longer."

Could you ask for a better recommendation for taking any drug than what was stated above? If you didn't know what he was talking about and you read this description of the benefits of taking a certain medication wouldn't we all rush out and buy a bushel of it? You have to admit it sounds like a miracle drug. Yet many of us still hold on to our old beliefs about the superstitions which we attribute to religious practice. Is it superstitious to be aware of the positive effects which religious belief has on our health both mental and physical? Is it then superstitious once we accept the scientific studies to concede that a belief in a higher power not only makes us happier but it makes us healthier and allows us to live a more satisfying life? It begins to sound like all those naysayers who testified to their own exalted intelligence in resisting the temptation to believe in a deity above themselves may not have been quite as smart as they figured themselves to be. Perhaps those of us who were deemed "dimwitted, less educated" that found some religious foundation in their lives may in fact have the last laugh, the ultimate reward.

Keeping the debate at a more "real life" level we have to take stock of the benefits on the material plane in a belief founded in the spiritual plane. If we keep the debate here among the findings of research scientists then we haven't at least from the outset alienated anyone. Although there will still be the argument that the belief in a God, the practice of a religion are merely mental concepts which prove nothing about the actual existence or non-existence of a divine being. That is definitely putting a fine point on the pencil and technically a valid argument. The problem with that argument, as with many arguments seeking to deny the existence of anything which cannot be proven through the scientific method, is that it has no substance of itself. In other words it derives all its life all its vitality from the destruction, the denial of a postulate which has scientifically proven objective evidence of its power for creating good and positive conditions.

Those who approach the destruction of spirituality through the rubric of science are trying to measure the distance between the galaxies with a teaspoon. Haven't we seen in our previous explorations of the various scientific questions that science does not even have the most basic answers to the fundamental questions besetting us? Scientists do not know what consciousness is, they do not know what

WILLIAM J. PARDUE

time is, they do not know how we all came to be in the beginning, they do not know what space is. Is our brain so determined and set on making itself the center of our universe and its jealousy of any other non rational competitor is complete and exclusive. In spite of the flashes of brilliance which our brain is either intrinsically capable of originating or capable of being conscious of despite their origination in some other undefined place, we are tied and bound to the rational mantra of our brains. We are slaves to the neural pathways which have been worn from use in the intricacies of our thinking organ. Our brains and the personal software which we have developed to cope with this existence lack the capacity to see beyond its own survival. We can of course leap over it, advance beyond its parameters but we must withdraw our mental energies from the micro management of everything which we touch and submit to a greater power, a greater intellect. After all we did not invent the universe. The extent of our scientific inquiry is to mimic, to discover, to uncover the inner workings of nature, the divine creation, the flow, the rule of life. We can only pick at the corners, nibble on the crumbs. We are not the creators of all we see and unless we are being less than truthful with ourselves we know there is some force out there which must be reckoned with whether we like it or not which is at the center of all that we witness. Of course our own inevitable death reminds us of the inconsequential space and time unit which we occupy during our brief and meteoric lives on this plane.

If we return then to the dilemma of what it means to discover that people with a religious belief enjoy this journey through life more intimately and thoroughly than those that do not hold such a belief. It could be explained in the context of "positive thinking" where the holding of a religious belief intrinsically bestows upon the believer a positive construct within which he can abide. The other possibility is as the author suggested in the article quoted above. It may not be the religious belief but the religious upbringing which causes the more positive characteristics of people who consider themselves believers. There was an implication in that article that the reason religiously minded individuals have better lives is that their habits, their mode of living preordains the positive results. Perhaps this concept can be better explained by an example I read in the newspaper the other day. The article mentioned that people who contested their traffic tickets by going to court were more likely to be in an accident or get another ticket shortly thereafter their appearance in court than those people who did not contest their ticket. There are many different reasons why this may have happened but it was postulated that it happened because people who participate in "risky" behavior are more likely to have accidents of whatever kind is associated with that risky behavior. Going to court to challenge a traffic ticket was seen as "risky" behavior and therefore the subsequent ticket/accident was a result of that continued risky behavior. Those who did not go to traffic court but merely paid their tickets were less likely to take risks and therefore less likely to have another accident.

This approach to discovering why people who "believe" in a religious sense seem to have a better quality and quantity of life than those who do not believe is intriguing. Is it reasonable to accept the premise that the benefits of a religious belief are to be found in the "behaviors" which are either encouraged or prohibited? Relating back to the concept of risky behavior results in consequences which are less predictable, more dire. Driving fast, driving without a seat belt, driving while intoxicated or under the influence are all high risk behaviors. They are all behaviors which in most religious circles are discouraged. If you consider the rules by which religious communities govern themselves starting with the Ten Commandments and branching out into the myriad array of rules and regulations which proscribe risky behaviors then you can understand the argument that a less hazardous, happier life may be a result of such practices. Adultery, drug use, worshiping false idols, stealing, lying, killing, hating, and all the other behaviors which are "risky" because of the causal relationship with negative results are prohibited by religious peoples. By practicing their religion and foregoing these behaviors the possibility of a happy life increases proportionately. There are those then who hypothesize that it is not a belief in "God" per se that creates the happiness quotient but the associated behaviors which are prohibited by the religion itself.

That argument however fails when the fact that "religious" people who are subject to stress are better able to manage their stress and be positive and happy despite difficult times. This example takes the merit away from the argument that lifestyle behaviors are the only benefits of the religious life. The example of equally stressed individuals, therefore people subject to negative factors which cause stress cope differently with the existence of stress in their lives. Here we do not have the avoidance of risky behavior and therefore the elimination of negative life situations which are associated with those behaviors but we have people in equal positions. We now have an effect due to religious belief which transcends the lack of risky behavior and instead dilutes, diminishes, eliminates the symptoms of negative consequences in our lives. A person who has lost their job, perhaps their home, who is going through a divorce, having trouble with their kids, their parents, their bosses, their spouses are the ones who will remain less agitated, more centered and happier if they have religious beliefs. This is really a good piece of news. There is a balm for our sorrows, our losses, our depressions and it is in the transformation of our mental geography so that a "mountain" of faith, of religious belief, rises above the horizon of our consciousness and gives us hope, imbues us with faith.

I think the real problem here for the spread of this "miracle cure" is our own mental intransigence. We cannot change our way of thinking absent a "critical mass" in our lives being experienced which makes us question the foundation upon which we have constructed our lives, our self concepts. A real life transformation requires a willingness to participate and desire to change and a fundamental shift in the center of gravity in our consciousness. The center must move away from us towards "God" a divine force which determines our fate, our destiny to the extent which we are willing to submit ourselves to it, to surrender our wills, at least long enough to experiment with the idea. Aside from that the basic fact which seems to be scientifically established is that a belief in a higher power makes us happier people. That is not a small feat in this raucous, bare knuckle, street brawling society which we find ourselves.

THE INTERVIEW,
SATAN'S REBUTTAL

If the devil could be persuaded to write a bible,
he would title it, "You Only Live Once."

Sidney J. Harris

It is only fair really in the context of a thorough investigation into the role of religion and the existence of God in our society to consider the role of Satan and his thoughts on all of this. It seems apparent that if one is proffering the existence of God, of great goodness, then the existence of Satan, must be given an equal right for what need be there for a God of goodness and light if there is no Devil no Prince of darkness and decadence as his counterpoint, his foil his reason to exist. Their coexistence is mutually dependent on each maintaining a presence and a character which defines their powers and their limitations if any. In fact without evil, as symbolized by Satan then God is without work to do, he is irrelevant. It was Satan who tempted Eve who then tempted Adam, or so the story goes.

We must keep in mind that the major significance of good and evil and God and Satan is that they both vie for the human soul, the spirit of man. Both of these supernatural entities have as their goal a recruitment of as many human souls as possible. The success of their efforts, the range of their influence is measured by the state of human affairs. The Bible foretells the "end of days" and the "judgment day" which is preceded by a viral decline of morality and righteous living by our species. The Bible therefore predicts the ultimate success of the Devil over God on our planet. Whether God and Satan are merely mythical allegories invented by man to describe "circumstances" of good or evil and their origin or if they are in fact real forces in this cosmic matrix with which we have to contend does not obviate our obsession with them. We as a species submit our questions of morality to these entities and live by the results of our choice. A hypothetical discussion with Satan may help to flush out the basic issues which must be resolved in determining the reality of God and the existence of good and evil and their genesis.

Lucifer replies

Q: How would you prefer that I address you?

A: I will submit to your preference.

Q: There are so many names, Satan, Devil, "The Deceiver" "The Prosecutor", Prince of the Earth, Prince of the Wind, Challenger, Lucifer, Light Bringer, Bringer of Enlightenment, The Accuser, Tempter of Jesus, Shaitan, The Opposer, Father of Lies, Father of Deceit, God of the Underworld, Prince of Darkness and many more.

A: Was there a question there?

Q: No, Just casting about for some sense of your preference.

A: My preference is whatever it is that makes you most comfortable. If you choose Deceiver or Father of Lies, however, I would caution you to more fully expound on your reasons for so doing.

Q. Is there some reason you take offense at these particular appellations?

A. Isn't it obvious?

Q. The only thing which would be obvious would be that you were being branded a liar when in fact you are not.

A. Excellent. I am merely the mirror of your soul. I only want what is best for you, what it is that makes you happy. If you consider that a lie then so be it. I take no position other than the fulfillment of the individual rights and expression of their desires here on Earth.

Q. What if that something which makes me happy is centered in a belief in God then what, are you still happy with my choice?

A. It is not about me being happy with your choice it is about you freely choosing a path without the necessity of measuring your decision against some "random" set of rules or laws which prohibit your choice before it is even made. I simply have only one concern and that is that you live your life fully and completely all the while keeping yourself at the center of that life using your time here on earth to obtain the fullest and most exceptional life possible. In order to do this you must bow to no other God than yourself. You must consider no other person besides yourself unless of course you willingly choose to do so because it gives you pleasure.

Q: What exactly does that mean to "bow to no other God than myself".

A: I believe that you already know what that means but I will explain. This life which you are living is the only one you will ever have. There is no heaven, no hell only these few precious years which you will exist as you know yourself now and then you will be gone forever extinguished, separated from the glorious emanations of life which you bask in each day you take a breath. You will be as a candle flame snuffed out with no further opportunities to experience yourself. If you accept that truth you will be forced to confront the further truth that you are then the maker of your own life experience, you are your own God with no other Gods above you. Any Gods which you might imagine exist only exist in your mind; they have no independent existence outside of your mind.

Q: Does anything have an independent existence outside of my mind?

A: After your parents died did everything that they ever knew cease to exist?

Q: Of course not but there were some things that they were conscious of which when they ceased to exist so did the consciousness of those things. Do you exist independently of my mind or are you also just a construct of my imagination?

A: I am the eternal profligate. I was here before this planet had a separate existence from the cosmos and I will be here after the last flicker of life is extinguished in the black void of space. I will witness the last moment of your life and every other soul who ever set foot on this planet. I will look them in their eyes and measure their souls. I will smell your fear and taste your terror as you evaporate into nothingness all the while waiting for your God to rescue you and when he doesn't you will know that I was right all the time, but then it will be too late for you. Your millisecond of existence in the infinity of time will have been spent and no trace of its former presence will remain.

Q: What is your purpose, why do you haunt mankind?

A: My purpose is to destroy all obstacles to the full and complete unadulterated, inexhaustible flow of life through the form of man into the universe. The only haunting that I do is fictional, created by religionists who pretend to know me and God and what we both want in relation to mankind. They have it all wrong for I am the real savior. I am the one who paves the way for truth for everyone's passionate, willful and absolute right to be themselves. After all even if you believe in God he gave you all those passions, those inclinations, those behaviors which mankind later characterized as bad. Why would he give them to you if he didn't mean for you to utilize them to their greatest extent?

Q: What exactly does that mean to be ourselves to the fullest?

A: It means that man came into being as the cosmic sensor through which the life force could experience itself in all its fullness. Man is a conduit through which it could fulfill its full potential. Man provides an amplification of the life force, an experiential magnifier making all experiences grander, deeper and more alive. Man is the instrument through which the life force plays its melodies, forms its creations and expresses its many moods. Man is the canvas and the life force is the artist. I am the procurer of the paints and I have the job of delivering a canvass which is clean of any obstructions, any defects or imperfections. These manmade Gods and their artificial rules for living are merely impediments to the full and complete expression of the life force. They are fictional barriers to the most complete expression of human emotions for the sake of the individual.

Q: Why is it that you exist and you contend that God does not exist? Isn't it imperative that if there is good there must be the counterpoint of evil and vice versa?

A: The operative word is "if". If God exists and he is the symbol of all that is good then that explains why I exist as a counterpoint. The problem with your question is that it contains a premise which is false. I am not evil; I am the agent of the life force which is the creator of all that you behold. There is no such thing as evil that too is a figment of the religious mind designed to aid in the recruitment of weak minded individuals to the flock of believers. It is my task to do as I have described. I simply remind people, like you, that to believe in a God of goodness is self hypnosis, nothing more and nothing less. Your belief is a crippling force which only inhibits the completeness of your instinctual drives, your natural desires. I embody everything that is good so why the need of something, someone else.

Q: This cosmic force which you continue to refer to that sounds a little bit like God is described. Have you ever considered the likeness between the two?

A: There are no similarities other than the powers of creation. The Cosmic Force flows with an unimpeded intensity into the universe transforming everything that it encounters. Your God flows from the individual mind as a mixed bag of incantations, chants, beads, commandments and ceramic statues. Your god can be held by the base and dropped on his head and he will break into a thousand pieces. My master, the cosmic force cannot be grasped, touched, or transcended in any form because it is all forms and infinite energy.

Q: This Cosmic Force is it a force with any conscience, any moral direction?

A: If you consider the force to conquer, to overcome, to possess, to assert, to subjugate, to animate all things in its power a force with a direction then the answer would be yes, it is a moral force.

Q: But you wouldn't consider it a moral force in the sense of conforming to a religious set of rules and regulations which prohibits certain behaviors and allows others?

A: What possible scenario could you concoct which would have the center of all creation bowing and submitting to the mere ephemeral dictates of any religion, all religions founded in the imagination of man. All the religions in the world, all the Gods ever created by man and all the believers who ever prayed to a power greater than them are like foolish children thinking that because they believe something strongly enough it must be real. The only moral prerogative is self fulfillment at the expense of all else.

Q: Does that mean to the exclusion of everyone else?

A: Of course it does what else would it mean. The Cosmic force wants each individual to manifest their inner most desires and inclinations to their fullest. By the very nature of that goal there will be other individuals who come between you and what you want. You then have the choice to either pursue your own desires, without thought of others or you capitulate to the emasculating knife of religious dogma and move out of their way, denying your own wishes and letting them get closer to theirs.

Q: That sounds like a recipe for total chaos and confusion. Does this cosmic force desire that mankind self destruct? Does it desire that there be total pandemonium?

A: You are a pessimist. You immediately assume that this freedom of choice allowed mankind will inevitably lead them to self destruction. Maybe you should open your mind to the possibility that only through complete, unimpeded individual expression can the ultimate truth of the creative force which governs us all be known. It is my job to bring enlightenment to mankind. Enlightenment is the total and complete manifestation of this creative force through the medium of individual men and women coming to fruition.

Q: Where is the conscience in all this self seeking?

A: There is no conscience, at least outside of the purview of doing what is best for you. Conscience is a mythical monitor of behavior created by religionists to control mankind. Once you believe that your behavior is "bad or wrong" based on a reference to rules established by some authority outside of yourself, you have taken the bait which the religionists have offered you. You are caught, hook, line and sinker with nowhere to go except back into the boat of religion where you flap around while you die an unnatural death.

Q: So you believe that mankind is better off without restraints as to conduct especially in relation to the affect it has on others?

A: I know that mankind is better off without restraints. I have been trying to get that point across since the beginning of time. Fear, Anger, Hate, Jealousy, Envy, Greed, Lust, War are all naturally arising manifestations of man's character. They are part of you because the universe needs a means of expressing those emotions. They all have their place in the retinue of emotions and they all serve their respective functions. It is alright to get mad and to show it. It is alright to hate someone because they have obviously done something to deserve your hatred. It is part of the cosmic design that mankind goes to war and kills his enemy.

Q: So then it is your role in this cosmic cauldron of enlightenment to ensure that mankind is allowed the total unimpeded expression of their individual desires?

A: That is correct.

Q But isn't it true that when each individual seeks to fully and completely express their passions that there will be a complete and total breakdown of the "community". Isn't it also fair to say that the community evolved as a means of taming human behaviors so that more people would be able to express themselves within the parameters of the community?

A: It is fair to say that, however, how successful has that been? Are you going to point to any particular culture, society or religion that has tamed mankind's most base desires and behaviors?

Q: Well there have been societies and religions both historically and now that have failed to tame their most destructive inclinations. There have always been others, however, that I have contained their individual desires and come to understand that serving the whole in the end benefits the individual. What could possibly be wrong with curbing your own animal impulses so that the group, the community could be safer for everyone. Is it right for a gang to terrorize a City, a neighborhood, a country? What about the rights of those they are terrorizing are they just forgotten?

A: It is clear that you have religious leanings. All this consideration for others is false posturing. You are created to have the opportunity to fully express yourself regardless of who it compromises. The suicide bomber is only expressing their rights to die in a public expression of their outrage against the enemy. The strong shall overcome the weak that is the rule of the Universe. Either you remain strong or you die, you die to yourself, to all that you deserve.

Q: If we get back to your description of this creative force which gives life to us all it sounds strikingly similar to what we conceive God to be. Is your cosmic force in fact only another pseudonym for God?

A: I believe that it is the other way around. God is another pseudonym for the cosmic force.

Q: So you would concede that this cosmic force has been mistaken for god and perhaps many other things as it is the mother of all creation. If it is indeed the mother of all creation and all creation which arises from it is to go unchecked then why would you restrict a belief in god if that too is a tendency?

A: A belief in God as practiced by mankind inevitably restricts behavior. All religions practice restrictions of some sort or another. The Catholics, Buddhists, Taoists, Hindus, Baptists, Protestants, Muslims, Jews, Mormons and even the Satanists all want to diminish the power of man. They want to drain his passions, poison his spirit of independence, eliminate his lust, stamp out his aggressive tendencies so that those who are less powerful, lesser individuals can compete, can rise to the top over the bodies of castrated warriors.

Q: Isn't your role of making sure that these tendencies, regardless of how bestial they may be are honored, are given their full complement of expression in our culture?

A: That is precisely what my goal is. I am the liberator of mankind. God is the jailer of mankind and he, as you define him, is dedicated to the eradication of every natural impulse towards self-aggrandizement. Man is the King of Beasts he must be allowed to howl, to kill, to hunt his prey and devour them or to love them as he wills. The seven deadly sins are his mantra, the sign of his excellence and the proof of his pedigree.

Q: What if we both agree that man has free will and that God is defined as the creative force that includes everything which we witness in the cosmos, not just the good but also the bad, the evil. Would you be willing to entertain that idea for the sake of argument?

A: Of course. I like nothing better than to enlighten the unenlightened about the true nature of God.

Q: Would you agree then that God, in whatever form he may take, has allowed mankind through free will to choose what part of God's creation he is most inclined to utilize for his own interests?

A: Yes and it is my job to let mankind know that there are no restrictions to those choices.

Q. But you have in fact restricted mankind's choices to only those which allow a complete and unedited expression of any and all instinctual proclivities. You boldly condemn the religionists for proselytizing yet aren't you at the vanguard of proselytizers beating the drums for unobstructed expressionism?

A: I am an advocate for complete and free expressionism. God, religion and behavioral dogmatism have a strangle hold on mankind. I am merely an agent of the cosmic creative force expressing freedom of choice.

Q: You mean freedom of choice as long as it does not involve a choice which may include restrictions on behavior, on impulses?

A: Restrictions on choices is not freedom of choice.

Q: Isn't a restriction on choices when made freely, when the alternative is also available for the choosing, isn't that freedom of choice? The alcoholic who chooses to restrict his drinking behavior voluntarily, because it transforms the quality of his life from bad to good, isn't he expressing his freedom of choice because he knows the consequences of following destructive instinctive behaviors, such as consuming too much alcohol?

A: He is but the only reason his choice to consume too much alcohol has led to less than happy circumstances is that society and religion has made it difficult through their laws and rules to be happy and be an alcoholic.

Q: So it is societies fault, the cultures fault for the alcoholic's quality of life? It has nothing to do with the person who chooses to poison his body and soul with alcohol.

A: That is right. The individual is the victim and society, cultures and religions are the culprits the victimizers.

Q: Well that is an interesting take on the matter. I appreciate your perspective on the benefits of pride.

A: Pride is the force that drives all major accomplishments. If you doubt that now, for I know that you have sworn allegiance to pride in your past, I will always be here with hand outstretched in a gesture of goodwill ready to accept you into the "enlightened" way of life when you realize the error of your ways.

Q: I have already walked your path and it took me to a dead end, however, when I reversed my direction back to God I recaptured my life with another chance to do right this time. I knew then that I had traveled far in the wrong direction but it only took a minute to turn around and I have celebrated that about face every day since. I was not able to make that turn, that transition until I understood the meaning of humility. Although I am just at the beginning of that road back I now realize that pride is what took me in the wrong direction and will hinder me from righting my course if I fail to conquer it.

The quiet conscience is an invention of the Devil
Albert Schweitzer

PRIDE,
THE GREATEST SIN OF ALL

Through pride we are ever deceiving ourselves.
But deep down below the surface of the
average conscience a still, small voice says to us,
something is out of tune.

Carl Gustav Jung (1875-1961)
Swiss psychologist and psychiatrist

Pride is defined by Dictionary.com as follows:

noun

1. a high or inordinate opinion of one's own dignity,
    importance, merit, or superiority, whether as cherished
    in the mind or as displayed in bearing, conduct, etc.
2. the state or feeling of being proud.
3. a becoming or dignified sense of what is due to oneself
    or one's position or character; self-respect; self-esteem.
4. pleasure or satisfaction taken in something done by or
    belonging to oneself or believed to reflect credit upon
    oneself: civic pride.
5. something that causes a person or persons to be proud:
    His art collection was the pride of the family.

It is difficult to look at this definition and honestly
assess how many of these traits I recognize in myself. It is
not a pleasant exercise nor is the result satisfying. It has the

effect of deflation of the ego, not a particularly comfortable feeling. It has the taste of sour wine, a wine which you used to cherish as your favorite. It is embarrassing to realize that pride is such a pervasive driving force, a momentum towards personal exaltation which reminds me of the old saying: "The one creature in all creation which the angels were most astonished by was the prideful man". As I write this I do not like the feelings which haunt me, the sense of pride laughing at my dullness, my dawning realization of an exaggerated and inflated fiction which I have lived. I understand intimately the workings of pride; however, I did not associate them with my behavior until only recently. The Emperor's New Clothes comes to mind as a perfect allegory of pride. The prideful man or woman does not see themselves, cannot see themselves as others see them because certainly if they did they would cease to be prideful. The Emperor with his new suit, which of course existed only in his imagination, walked among his subjects and saw only in their eyes their great admiration for his glorious and magnificent suit of clothes. The Emperor was never conscious of his own nakedness but only of his pride in the magnificence of his public exhibition. He saw only admiration where there was only astonishment.

It makes me wonder about our capacity to understand ourselves, this scene with the emperor. We all see pride everyday in others but it is so much more difficult to see in ourselves. Pride is an asset in our culture, in this world of material illusions. It is admired. It is cherished for what it represents. Success, accomplishment, superiority, intelligence, skill, power are all the characteristics which we associate with pride. Personal pride, however, carries other traits and consequences. Arrogance, selfishness, greed, lust, envy, hatred, spite and lack of conscience are all siblings of pride and they can be found wherever pride resides. Pride knows no boundaries, it knows no rules and it obeys no higher authority than itself. It is blind, deaf and dumb to the world around it and considers no other persons or things to be equal to it in stature. Why has pride taken such a central role in our culture? Can't we see the results of prideful behavior? Wouldn't it be better to admit our faults, our culpabilities, our shortcomings and work on them than parade through the streets denying their existence when they are in clear sight of all? A summary of Hans Christian Andersen's Story of the Emperor's new clothes would be helpful to illuminate the vagaries of pride.

A long time ago there was an emperor who was obsessed with clothes. He had a new wardrobe for every hour of every day and he spent countless hours in his wardrobe closet admiring his enormous collection of clothes. This emperor enjoyed displaying his clothes through the streets of the city and watching the envy in the eyes of his subjects at the beauty of his clothes. It happened that two strangers arrived in town that held themselves out as weavers of cloth and fashioners of clothing extraordinaire. They claimed to be able to weave an extraordinary cloth which had exquisite texture and pattern. Even more amazing than that was this particular cloth was invisible to all persons who were either not suited for their office or unpardonably stupid. The emperor heard about this cloth and the astounding attribute it had of distinguishing the unfit and stupid from the wise and deserving citizens of his realm.

The emperor being the clothes aficionado that he was had to have such a suit made from this amazing cloth. The emperor commissioned the two strangers, who were actually impostors, intending to deprive the emperor of a small fortune, to weave this wardrobe. The two men demanded gold, fine cloth and set up two looms to start the process of weaving this incredible garment. As the work continued the emperor sent his own weavers to view the garment and inform him of its progress. Of course the weavers when shown the progress of the garment saw nothing. They could not however admit that they saw nothing because they knew this would mark them as unworthy of their offices or just plain stupid. They reported to the emperor that the clothes were progressing beautifully. So a parade of the emperor's agents visited the looms and all reported the same progress. Even the emperor visited the loom and although he saw nothing he could not admit it. So the emperor removed all his clothes was dressed in his invisible wardrobe and paraded through the streets. All his subjects knowing the significance of not being able to see the clothes expressed their astonishment at the beauty of the emperor's new garments. Finally a child called out that in fact the emperor was naked and when he did the emperor realized that the truth of the child's statement. The whole crowd realized it too and called out his nakedness.

The emperor knowing that they were right also realized that he was in the middle of the procession and he carried on with his servants in attendance as if he was in possession of the most beautiful suit imaginable, head high and carriage straight.

I had not thought of this story until I thought of pride. When I was young it was just an amusing story but now I see it as a profound revelation of the absurdity of pride. We also have our "new clothes" and we walk around with them basking in the admiration which we read in the eyes of others as they view our magnificence. The clothes could be your perceived superiority of intellect, inescapable beauty, engaging personality, profound knowledge and a vast store of wealth, refined spirituality, esteemed religiosity, position of power, or any other attribute which you believe you possess which sets you above your fellow man. Some people possess higher degrees of some attributes than others but in fact we all possess some distinct feature which may set us apart from others. The problem becomes when our "new clothes" whatever we might imagine them to be, make us special, set us above others, bestow privileges on us which others cannot enjoy. Our "new clothes" invigorate our sleeping pride. They destroy community, they set one against the other, they mock God's creations and they terrorize the truth.

The Devil was once a treasured angel of God, or so the story goes, but his pride got the best of him. How many stories do we read in the newspaper about men and women who have fallen victim to their pride? There is always a story about some political leader, some movie star, some financier, some sports hero, who has been parading in his invisible set of "new clothes" when a child yells or the crowd yells that he is naked, his clothes do not exist. A fall from the steepest heights of pride is devastating. The realization of our nakedness after so much parading and pretending is a lesson in humility. It is a percipient moment when we have an opportunity to turn to some higher authority, some spiritual guidance outside of ourselves for forgiveness of our own stupidity, our own failure to be worthy of our station in life. It is a moment which can define our lives, a moment which can liberate us from our own grandiosity and ignorance. It can bring us into the light, into the community of mankind where self aggrandizement is not commendable.

This can be a moment of extreme self realization. It is no doubt a painful moment, a momentarily debilitating moment, but it can be a door to self knowledge. Once through that door we can see ourselves more clearly, we can take our own measure, a measure which we can see and experience, not an invisible moment. It is not the same moment which the Buddha had under the fig tree but it is a transformative moment of lesser degree but of immeasurable significance in setting our life course right or weighing in on the quality of our lives.

In considering pride and mankind and the influence one has on the other it is a puzzling matter. Why it is that man has such a difficult time perceiving his persona, his self which others see so clearly? What is it about pride that we all cherish it, seek it, and flaunt it every chance we have? It does make us feel, at least momentarily or for as long as the feeling sustains itself, that we are superior to our peers. It marks us out as different by virtue of whatever it is which we believe we possess which others do not, or at least do not in the quantities which we possess it. Pride also attracts the attention of others. Even if they question the high status which we bestow upon ourselves they are drawn towards the confidence, the show of strength and certainty which is manifested by the prideful man. They are drawn to the power which it generates, the invulnerability which is exuded. Pride is grown and nourished carefully from within our psyches. We waste nothing that can be used to make it grow and flourish. A word, a look, a trophy, your name heard in a passing conversation are all fertilizers, mulches, can all be used to enrich the soil of our minds wherein we grow our pride. Pride, however, takes on a life of its own. At some yet indefinable point in its growth it becomes a free agent. It becomes our master and when that happens it blinds us to its evil methods and we abide by its ways because at the end of the day pride is the ultimate drug. It makes us feel alive, it makes us feel powerful. We feel justified in all we do because pride tells us that we are. A fight with pride is a fight with the jealousy of Satan, the envy of Lucifer. The small incessant voice from the Dark Prince who lives within us encourages our pride, our arrogance as our due, our right.

Of course as with anything else a blanket condemnation is seldom a just or fair assessment of anything, even pride.

There are brands of pride which can be positive. The pride of a parent in the experience of their child who has grown into a loving, productive and enlightened member of society is to be encouraged. Pride which has the potential to encompass all peoples thereby not excluding anyone because of their particular characteristics is not harmful. There is a pride, however, which manifests division, envy, hatred and all things malignant to our society. That pride was already part of the definition which was set forth above.

"A high or inordinate opinion of one's own dignity, importance, merit, or superiority, whether as cherished in the mind or as displayed in bearing, conduct, etc." There is also a list of behaviors which indicate a prideful demeanor which is exclusive, condemnatory of others and superior. This brand of pride is our nemesis, our cancer, our downfall. See if you can identify any of these behaviors which you may be personally familiar with. This list was taken from the internet site by Robert Leroe speaking on humility and pride.

1. To think that what one says or does is better than what others say or do
2. To always to want to get your own way
3. To argue with stubbornness and bad manners whether you are right or wrong
4. To give your opinion when it has not been requested or when charity does not demand it
5. To look down on another's point of view
6. Not to look on your gifts and abilities as lent
7. Not to recognize that you are unworthy of all honors and esteem, not even of the earth you walk on and things you possess

8. To use yourself as an example in conversations
9. To speak badly of yourself so that others will think well of you or contradict you
10. To excuse yourself when you are corrected
11. To hide humiliating faults from your spiritual director, so that they will not change the impression they have of you
12. To take pleasure in praise and compliments
13. To be saddened because others are held in higher esteem
14. To refuse to perform inferior tasks
15. To seek to stand out
16. To refer in conversation to your honesty, genius, dexterity, or professional prestige
17. To be ashamed because you lack certain goods

I know that when I first read this list I was uncomfortably familiar with many if not all of these examples. I never considered them to be prideful only "the way things are". I never thought they were anything but an assertive and confident nature taking its rightful place in the moment. If I was so blind to the real nature of these actions, to the insipid, stupid and obnoxious pride which I exhibited even though my "magnificent suit was invisible" and even the children noticed it, cried out my nakedness. It is embarrassing now to think about those times when I walked naked among the crowd holding my head high, even haughty, while the angels were astonished by the pride of man. The old saying that "pride precedes the fall" is as true a recipe for self annihilation as it ever was.

Why is it that this particular brand of pride has been a curse on our species? Why are we so drawn to an "inordinate opinion of our own dignity, importance, merit or superiority"? We know that we are. We see it every day that we step outside into the day and perhaps we live with it in our homes. Individuals, all of us at times, who display behavior which exudes self importance, arrogance, disdain towards others. This is the stuff wars are made of. This is the seed of greed, lust, hatred, genocide, lack of conscience, and most things evil which we can imagine. It cannot be constructive because by its nature it is exclusionary, condemnatory, dismissive, heartless behavior. Unless we learn to control and recognize our prides then we are doomed as a species for of all our animal behaviors, it is the most destructive and it is the single defining behavior of our species which makes us the most vicious and dangerous of all our animal brethren.

HUMILITY,
THE ANTIDOTE TO PRIDE

What makes humility desirable is the marvelous
thing it does to us; it creates in us a capacity for
the closest possible relationship with God."

Monica Baldwin

Pride's first child is the "right" to disregard authority,
others rights, rules and to cheat, steal, lie, and revel
in our own glorious selves to the disadvantage of all who
are unlucky enough to come into contact with us. It is the
ultimate exemption from all accountability for any personal
actions and their consequences. It is a royal entitlement, in
the character of Henry VIII, which answers to no person,
supplicates to no God. It is the heart of every war, every
act of violence which begins in justification and ends in
annihilation of those who threaten our pride, who would
dare to shout out that we are naked.

The remedy to pride is humility. It is a word which man,
the proudest of animals, finds distasteful. A trait which he
can find no benefit in unless of course it is displayed in his
enemy, his adversary and then it is seen as justified under
the law of God and man. Humility is held in great scorn
by our winner take all rules of engagement for how can
anyone who is willing to let the next guy step over him

win anything. It is not possible we imagine. Besides it may have been alright for Jesus and other historical figures who manifested this self effacing trait and by so doing earned themselves a place in the spiritual history of mankind but there is really no place for it today we might argue. The conundrum for us is why we would possibly choose the lesser over the greater, a cottage over a mansion, a janitor's job over a doctor, a Kia over a Mercedes. The choices seem obvious until you have the opportunity to make them and live with the consequences. Many people never have the opportunity to make these choices and therefore the reality of the choice is non-existent except for what they see on television. Those who have had the experience to upgrade, move up, choose the greater over the lesser know that the greater is not always the choice that brings happiness. There are countless stories of lottery winners who after winning millions of dollars and buying everything that they had been told would make them happy spiral into a course of self destruction.

The citizens of the United States of America rank only sixteenth in happiness in the other nations of the world. Nigeria on the other hand which has an annual income of approximately three hundred dollars ranks higher in personal happiness than any other country. How is that possible? They do not have the possessions, the stature, the material "dazzle" which we have, which are emblems of our pride. They also do not consume one hundred and twenty million prescriptions of anti depressants every year. There is a disconnect here. We have been told, we have been promised, that hard work will lead to more affluence which will lead to greater happiness. This doesn't seem to be proven by the evidence. The question has to be asked if we have been sold a "bill of goods" an "elixir of consumerism" as a cure all for any ailment which we might have or imagine we have. As one of the richest nations in the world with a standard of living envied by the vast majority of the world's population we are living in a drug induced coma of consumerism, of materialism which fails to fulfill its promise of salvation, happiness and eternal peace.

Is this religion of "spending to make us important" any different than any other religion which preaches abstinence for salvation. There really is no difference between the two. They both are merely arguments, worlds constructed of words which work their magic on our consciousness capturing it only to use it to further feed the wildfire of unquenchable desires. While the Devil captures souls to caste into hell, the "golden calf of consumerism" consumes our souls while we are still alive, drains the spiritual vitality from the core of our being and turns us into drug swilling robots. In the end we stand swaying from the blow, just as our nation does now, wondering how it all came to this. We only remember the promises which now taste like sawdust on our palates. They are like lies told to us as children are told "white lies" to make them behave, to keep them in line. Is everybody lying to us? Is there any way out of this debacle, this melt down of everything we held important, inviolable.

WILLIAM J. PARDUE

We must all realize by now that pride is not the answer; neither is being right at the expense of the other guy being wrong. We are struggling, as a nation, with the greatest crisis of our time. Despite what is said about the great depression, this is worse and what do our leaders do to assist the people in their time of need. They point fingers at each other. They accuse the other of being radical, ridiculous, and outlandish, if only they were as smart as we are (there goes that pride again) then they would certainly see the error of their ways. So this argument goes, the Christians versus the Muslims, the republicans versus the democrats, the vegetarians versus the carnivores and on and on. Our society has been decimated by factions. Factions which do not have the ability to make sound arguments based on the merits of their positions so they must attack the other side. They must brand the other side as irrational, unreasonable and un-godly so that it is easier to hate them, to annihilate them, to justify wars, genocide and other atrocities against the opponents. The misguided opponents who fail to see our new suit of clothes and instead believe that we are naked. How ignorant of them, it just proves their lack of intelligence or wisdom of proper upbringing. We cannot believe that they fail to be convinced by the web of words which we spin around them, aren't they listening, don't they believe in God.

I have noticed, especially in the last year the number of people that come into my office or that I see in their places of business or leisure who are completely and totally frustrated with their leaders from all walks of life but especially

316

the political leaders. Pride has a large role in creating this dissatisfaction. A little humility on both sides would go a long way towards mending the tears in our society which have created this mess which we find ourselves faced with. Is it too much to ask these proud leaders from all walks of life to allow enough humility into their lives so that they can admit that they may not in fact have the final answers to all questions of import? Is it too much to ask, that through a show of humility on both sides, the real problems can be addressed not just the self created problem of blaming and finger pointing. Are we not intelligent enough as a species that we will destroy ourselves in a nuclear cat fight over whose pride will prevail? Our frustration as a people is the inability for our leaders, our nation, to overcome a pride which is destroying us.

It is also a problem with us as individuals, this pride and this arrogance of aggression which destroys all non believers in its path. I know this arrogance of pride intimately and I believe that if you are honest with yourself you too will acknowledge that you have wielded the sword of pride against those who dared to claim that they could not see our suit of new clothes. The problem with humility is that it is so difficult to surrender to the knowledge of our own limitations. We want to know everything and be everything. We want to have all the answers when in reality we have very few and those we have change frequently and we fail to keep up with those changes. Our attitude of unrelenting pride promises to keep us safe from the enemy, from death, when all it does is deliver the knife into the hands of the enemy who then patiently and deliberately slips it between our ribs and into our very souls.

It is smart to be humble, to admit mistake, to own up to a weakness because it moves beyond the problem and into the solution. The only cost has been a slightly bruised ego, a momentary loss of face. This same pride has taken the reality of God and shredded it into a thousand pieces, each of which may contain some of the reality of God but none of which contain the entire reality of God despite their claims.

WHERE DO WE FIND GOD
AND WHAT DOES
HE LOOK LIKE

God is a circle whose center is everywhere and
circumference nowhere.

Voltaire (1694-1778)
French writer and historian.

I had an acquaintance tell me a story about his wife. She had been very sick for a few years. She had to be in hospitals, nursing facilities and needed constant care and attention. The story was told to me a few days after her death at a relatively young age. The day of her death he awoke to find a white dove on his windowsill. He had never seen a white dove outside of captivity and he certainly had not seen one around his house. He commented that this particular dove seemed to be looking directly at him, not like most birds that will not make direct eye contact for any period of time if at all but instead will look away, avoid a staring contest. That white dove was there all day. It seemed content to just be there as if waiting for something or someone. He did an internet search on white doves and found a reference to the Holy Spirit. The question is, was this white dove an agent of God and was it the Holy Spirit attempting to communicate with this man? The man's wife died that evening and the white dove was gone.

I believe that God or the Cosmic Ruler, or Supreme Life Force is constantly sending us messages, showing us signs to guide us, to let us know there is some force in this universe of ours which is beyond our comprehension. There is a force that cares enough about us to communicate if we are only conscious enough to hear it, to see it. Our pride is the biggest obstacle to finding this force, this Godhead, because pride blinds us to everything but its own desires. The first clue to finding out where God is can be answered at least in part by finding out what attitude has to be maintained in order to find where God is, where this cosmic unifying and life giving force emanates from.

It is clear to me that an attitude of pride cannot lead to a successful search for God's whereabouts. Our consciousness cannot simultaneously focus on different issues at the same time. When we are truly searching for something we are most successful when our search is focused and concentrated on the object of our desire. The choice of the object of our search necessarily precludes the search for other potential conflicting objects. Searching for reasons to justify our actions necessarily precludes finding that our actions were in fact unjustified. Searching for means to make more money will often preclude finding happiness. Searching for ways to make other people like us will often eliminate the possibility of finding ways to like ourselves. Holding fast to a prideful attitude will eliminate the possibility of finding humility which will doom the search for God. Pride is an absolute firewall to finding the reality of God. Pride takes the place of God. There is no need for a God when pride reigns supreme. God has no place here, he has nothing to do, no soul to heal. It only when pride stumbles against the curb of reality and falls to the ground is there a chance of redemption of spirit a resurrection of the willful and intentional search for a power greater than us. In order to find God we must suffer a failure of pride to redeem us, to protect us from the unknown.

The main difference between pride and humility is that pride is unearned (at least the false pride of which we are talking). A prideful attitude is often an invention of our imagination spun from invisible cloth without any substance in reality. Anyone can manufacture a reason for a prideful front and we are encouraged to do that in our current culture. Humility on the other hand is earned. Very few of us seek humility but by its very nature it is visited upon us often quite suddenly but always rudely and painfully. We have earned every ounce of humility which we have experienced such that the scales of pride and humility always remain balanced. Humility is paid for by the exchange of pride in equal amounts. I often think of a young man whom I saw for only ten minutes and I believe to this day that what he did was the bravest act which I had ever witnessed.

It was lunchtime and I had left the office to travel to the nearby Sizzler Steak House for lunch. The line was long that day and I found my place in the back of it not paying any particular attention to anyone in line. I finally tuned my consciousness to my surroundings and immediately noticed the back of the person standing in front of me with his back to me. He was of average height, with a slight build but neatly dressed. There was, however, something strange about his head its dimensions didn't seem exactly right but his hair was longer and somewhat full so it was difficult to determine. I had not been there long when he turned and I saw his profile. I have to mention that other people in line in front of me appeared nervous around him; they seemed to be looking at him surreptitiously, curiously. His profile presented a face that was grossly distorted in all its characters of his skull. The movie of the elephant man immediately came to mind and this young boy had the same misshapen features as that movie character. My heart silently cried out to him. The rejection of his deformity registered in everyone's eyes it created an uneasiness which hung heavy in the air. I was closest to him and when we made eye contact I saw the young man that he was behind that mask which was his face and it was a young man of innocence, a tortured soul but I also saw determination and the fullness of his courage. The young girl behind the counter could not hide her disgust nor could she resist an evil twisted smile which drew up one corner of her mouth as she watched him approach next in line. The disdain which she poured on him with her look, her evil smile made me cringe and I was standing behind him.

If I had my eyes closed when I heard him ask her for an application for the job which they advertised he sounded like any other teenager looking for a summer job, a way to make money perhaps to pay for dates. His voice was unwavering, slightly hesitant but firm in his intention to do what he had so courageously set out to do. The young girl behind the counter could not control her show of incredulity at his request. He took the application from her outstretched hand, thanked her and moved quietly out the door without looking back at the other patrons who followed him with their gazes until he disappeared forever into the world which tortured him but could not subdue his spirit.

This boy knew the meaning of humility. I often wonder if he cursed God each day of his life or if he prayed to God asking him for some answers, some reason for his condition. That is an answer I will never have. I do know that he had not given up hope of a life despite his deformity. This promised hope which was kindled by some thought, some idea which he held and which gave him courage, more courage than I would have had under the same circumstances. I always think of him as the bravest person I have met. As I reflect on that encounter now I wish I had an opportunity to speak with that young man again. We could all learn a lot from him. I would have sought the source of his courage that defied the ridicule of society which did not recognize that a young man inhabited that body, a boy with ambitions, hopes, dreams, and beyond all else courage and humility.

I like to think now that I have had this spiritual rebirth that this young man knew something about "God" which lifted him above us all and gave him a gift of spiritual insight which was uplifting. Those are just my wishes they may not

WILLIAM J. PARDUE

have anything to do with that young man but there was something he knew which I did not and it still inspires me when I think about it.

> "We need to find God and he cannot be found in noise and restlessness. God is the friend of silence. See how nature, trees, flowers, grass grows in silence. See the stars, the moon and the sun how they move in silence. We need silence to be able to touch souls"
>
> Mother Teresa

In order to find God we must first be looking for him with the right attitude. "Seek and you shall find". The question is, if you have the right attitudes, say humility and hope, where is the best place to find God? The place that first comes to mind is a church, synagogue, temple or other place of worship. Most of us first encountered the concept of God in such holy places. It seemed as children that these were the only places that you could actually contact him and that he was only available on holy days. The rest of the week presumably he would sit around in church waiting for the worshipers to return the next week to honor him. He was being held captive by grand stone and colored glass cathedrals, or clapboard churches. He was tied up inside those places of worship with ropes made of rituals and rules. This God who created the entire Universe held captive by Bibles, Korans, Torahs and other holy writings. How he must chafe at the restrictions, the tightness of the ropes the inability to move to breathe, to create. He also seemed to lack the ability

324

to speak directly to his sheep, his flock. He required priests, rabbis, monks, and other holy men to speak for him and to translate our wishes and hopes to God through them. We had no direct access to God. We were not sufficiently holy; we had not been trained properly.

Direct communication with God was for the learned, men of the book, men who held the secrets of God. We learned this as children and in many cases continued to believe it as adults. I listen to the sermons and they are full of how God wants us to live. They are bursting with admonitions as to what food to eat, beverage to drink, when to go to church, when to pray, how to pray, and generally a rule for every facet of our lives. The ultimate secret of all these sects is that there "way" is the best way or in some cases the only way to experience God, to be saved from our own sinful natures.

I often wonder how it is that this God who created all things and rules his creation with a compassionate and loving nature has been so decimated by well meaning souls who only had the interest of spreading the "word" of God over the face of the earth. The omniscient creator of the universe whose reach touched the outer limits of the known and unknown universe was pickled and canned, put on the shelf for consumption on Sundays. The various dominations, religious groups, and organized religions throughout history have stultified the cosmic deity by making him palatable to the people, by making him in the image of man. A living God cannot be found in a jar of pickled peppers. This being, this force which we pay such great reverence to is everywhere, in everything, and does not retreat to the hallways of only one sect, one religion and one system of beliefs. He is all and in us all, everywhere and everything if we take the time to look, to focus on the quest.

I was raised as a Catholic on the East Coast. It was church service every Sunday, every holiday and catechism it seemed every other day. A child understands very little about God but he is taught a great deal about religion. At the youngest age religion is pushed into their minds, molded into their heads where it remains for a lifetime. It requires an adult perspective to understand the immensity of the God concept. As a child he is just a good natured grandfatherly figure who protects us through the priests who bless everything which we own. The ceremony was high drama with smoking pots, chanting priests, Latin as the language of choice and the vast emptiness of the cathedral ceilings which were built sturdy and secure to hold God within its walls. The rituals of confession, confirmation, and communion were little more than theatre with little evidence of the presence of God. I can honestly say that I never experienced anything which I could associate with God until I became an adult and then those experiences were fleeting and often mistaken for good luck, or a propitious alignment of the planets. I left that Church as many people in my generation did. My reason was because it practiced only archaic rituals that contained no hint of a living and breathing God within them. They were a sign of God and symbol of his power and omniscience but for all the drama it was only a sign it was not the real thing. It was the tip of the tail of the tiger peeking out from the jungle fauna. You never saw the tiger, you never heard his roar, or felt his hot breath on your neck. You could not go to church and feel God's presence, speak with him directly because too many other people were speaking for him.

I also attended tent revivals in the South. This was a totally different experience with people yelling, shaking, falling down and running around the church while being possessed by the spirit of God. It was much different than the Catholic approach but more alive, more real and it felt like God could come and go as he liked. The tent had no doors, no stone walls to contain him. The worshipers didn't speak Latin but did speak in tongues which was as foreign as Latin. They seemed to be possessed by some spirit which animated and contorted their bodies and their language so that it mesmerized the viewer. It made you question whether or not God was really present, whether or not his spirit flowed through the congregation moving them like wheat in a thunderstorm.

I am indebted to organized religion in that they gave me the concept of God. They created the vehicle through which I first learned about the possibility of the existence of a God who had created all that we see and who had certain rules that must be followed. Organized religion does fulfill this role in our society regardless of how restrictive their particular practices are they announce the presence of a cosmic deity. Without that introduction discovering God for ourselves would be much more difficult. The difficulty with organized religions is that they are exclusive for the most part and critical of other sects for the other part. Any God who I could conceive of would not be exclusive for we are all his creations and we all ultimately share in the creation which has arisen from the cosmic source.

I am most comfortable with the Tao, the way of life philosophy which suggests a "way" which cannot even be spoken of and if it is spoken of then it is not the "way". The "way" suggests a flow of life, a movement of creation which responds to certain attitudes and actions of man. It cannot be grasped intellectually and it cannot be reduced to words. It can only be discovered by living and experimenting with behaviors which do or do not converge seamlessly with the flow of life and thereby do or do not create peace and harmony. It is referred to as the watercourse way, the flow of water, the flight of the bird in the sky, unpredictable in the rational sense of tracing trajectories yet "knowable" from a spiritual perspective. It is the womb of all life from which we and all things living emerge.

Our search for God must be daily and continuous. Search in this context means consciously seeking him, watching for the signs, the people who bring his message into our lives, and the events which clarify directions. It also means having faith that he exists. Faith has taken a bad rap and often communicates some cultish fixation practiced by religious extremists. It also smells of witchcraft, magic, and ignorance. When you consider faith more closely, more intimately it is none of the above. Faith calls God out of hiding for us.

God is sitting next to us on the park bench, he is rooting through the trash bins looking for cans and he is baking bread and building homes. He is in our midst every day of our lives sometimes in our faces and other times watching us from a distance but still always watching. He is always within earshot, listening for our call, our entreaty, our sobbing and heartbreak, our love and our joy. His love envelopes us and yet we are too busy to savor it. He is eternally patient for he has all the time there ever will be or ever was and we have but the briefest of moments. We are like fireflies that God watches and ponders as we blink in and out of existence. He is drawn to us by our faith for it is the clarion call which beckons him to our side, which allows him to enter the circle of our will and soften it, mold it and transform it into a perfect tool in his hands.

Real faith is an intentional decision by an individual to practice a hint of humility and adopt a working hypothesis that there exists a "ruling force" in the universe which can be identified and tested. We practice faith every day. We believe without hesitation, assuming good health that we will survive the day, pursue our activities and be here again tomorrow morning and we plan our life based on this faith based belief. We have faith that if we are "good people" who work hard we will be rewarded. We believe that when we say our wedding vows we mean them forever and we act on that belief, that leap of faith. We believe that if we are successful in a material sense then we will be happy. We believe that if we follow the rituals of materialism and practice them faithfully that they will bring us wealth and happiness. We believe that our government is there to serve us not us to serve it. We have faith that those in power will conduct themselves in such a manner that their actions will benefit the majority of people. We believe that man is the most intelligent of all life forms and that eventually he will solve all our problems merely by the application of his intellect.

If we all share these beliefs, a faith in these particulars and we understand as we read them that perhaps our belief, our faith is misplaced yet goes unquestioned, why do we hesitate to add God to the list of things we have faith in? Have we come to a point in our evolution when we have more faith in the electricity working in the morning when we awaken than we do in the reality of a God? Has the pickled God which religionists sell out of the back of their wagons been so diluted that there is no longer any semblance of the real center of life left. Do we all assume that this packaged "God" which is sold to us is all there is to God. This God who through the interpreters in the cathedrals and houses of worship promises everlasting life, a happy life in exchange for vowing allegiance to the religious strictures of their sect. This God who claims only one faith as the real faith yet each faith claims theirs as the "one".

Is it any wonder that we have grown weary, skeptical of this "child's god", this God who we met as children who is one dimensional, who lacks depth, lacks the passion and complexity that a cosmic deity would most certainly possess. We see the death, destruction, infidelity, genocide, atrocities, disasters, injustice around us and we wonder, we feel that our image of God stored in our consciousness from our earliest years has failed us. His self designated representatives have fashioned him in their own image. They have foisted there shriveled relic of God on us and declared him as their own. Our faith must be one which is rooted in a desire to know the living God, the Supreme life force which governs us all. This we must accomplish as individuals either within a community of like-minded individuals or alone with our own thoughts, our own desires fueled by our own faith.

When we finally know God, Who is he

> I fear one day I'll meet God, he'll sneeze and I
> won't know what to say.
>
> Ronnie Shades

The funny thing about it is you have already met him and he sneezed and you may or may not have said "bless you". There is a lot of talk about God's angels but in reality God is his angels, he is not just in his angels, he did not just create his angels, he is his angels. God is also man, and woman and child. He is not just in us he is us. We are part of his wholeness the fullness of his being, his creation. All living things are manifestations of God and integral working parts of God's being. God is everything we see. He is not just "good" although he is always loving the definition of "good" is subjective and what is good on one day is not so good on another. He is perfect in his execution of each and every detail of this spontaneous combustion of life forms which engulfs us and which we are not capable of understanding but only appreciating if we let ourselves. It is hard to imagine this endless parade of forms marching from birth to death as part of an orchestrated whole. A reflection on the current theory of the creation of the universe begins with a single form, perhaps a spherical ball pulsating in a place of nothingness until it bursts forth like a nuclear bomb the size of the universe itself and we all are catapulted from its womb alongside our siblings riding the wave of life into the edges of the Universe. We are all of us God, not any God but the God. If God were the ocean then we would be a drop of water in that vast Godness. The ocean itself is but a drop of water in the vast unknowable ocean we call God. The whole is greater than the sum of its parts. We are all part of God but God is much greater than the sum of all his creation.

Knowing God and finding him is not always a pleasant experience. He practices tough love. He can create vast destruction in your life. He can rob you of your most treasured gifts. He can leave you alone on the mountaintop gasping for air. The God of the Bible was frightening. He brought plagues, he told his people what he expected of them and if they failed to perform according to God's wishes they felt the wrath of God. Is it really so different today? Are we suffering both personally and communally as expiation for our wrongs committed? Have we attempted to look first within ourselves to answer the question of why some catastrophe was visited upon us? It is really just a question but the answer cannot be had until we accept responsibility for every act which we perpetrate during our lives. If you could imagine all of your acts having a life of their own and even though you are finished with them they remain in your circle of influence until such time as they can be nullified, balanced by their opposites. A perfect unity of acts, balanced precisely on the center of God's forehead.

The exercise which needs to be done to find God is the one of detail. We all know that there are certain exercises which develop certain muscles in the body. The curls develop the biceps, the dips develop the triceps and the crunches develop the abdominals. Well the exercise of paying attention to "the details in our lives" is the exercise which develops our God muscles. Our lives are hectic in 2011 and it seems like each year they get even more hectic, time becomes compressed so that a month feels like a week has passed. No time to rest, to think, to ponder, to entertain god. Any exercise which can reach God must carefully navigate our lack of time, our hurry, our rush to death. The first part of the exercise is to become vigilant. This means to become aware of what is happening around while it is happening. It is a focused awareness of our environment. The warm-up for this exercise is to focus on the "details". Let me give you some examples.

Cleaning up messes is perfect for this exercise. Starting with your own messes is a good first set. Don't leave water standing on the bathroom sink after you have used it. Examine the sink see if there is any standing water even a drop and if there is clean it up and put everything right. Keeping your car clean inside and out is good practice. Doing the work that has been assigned to you and doing it with an attitude that it is yours to do. Completing the work in a fashion which you can step back and admire is a great exercise. Finishing anything completely is always a blessing to someone. Hastily rushing a task and leaving it half done is a curse to someone always. If you drop a piece of paper on the floor, on the sidewalk, stop and pick it up. It is your responsibility, it happened on your shift and you were in charge of everything that happened on your shift. When you can master that simple attention to detail your whole life will improve. There will be no task too big for you or too difficult. The most difficult task is the one in the beginning, forcing you to pay attention to the detail, make everything right before moving on. You know if you fail to fulfill your obligations with regards to the details in your life then you and someone else will suffer because of it. A perfect world is obtained by people attempting to be perfect.

The family that faces the death of a child in an auto accident may have to face the fact of his culpability in that accident. His lack of attention to details may have cost him his life. Often times it is just that, lack of attention to detail, which creates our problems which plague us. How many stories have you read about the tourist who stood too close to the high surf which swept him off the rocks, or the baby which crawled out the third story window, or the infant left in the car with the window closed on a hot day. All of these are problems were created by a lack of attention to detail, by haste, by distracted thinking, by failure to do what is expected of you in the moment to make that moment perfect. You see the planets, the stars, the moon they leave no mess behind them, they know intimately the details of their orbits and maintain them religiously.

Of course this begs the question as to whether there are any accidents in life or at least accidents which cannot be traced to some one's lapsed consciousness at a crucial moment when death or destruction or embarrassment was just waiting for such a lapse. It is difficult to take a position with ourselves that we must practice perfection in our lives. Perfection here means a maximum effort to be responsible for all acts in our lives and their consequences. I have a propensity to drive too fast and yet every time I get a ticket I blame the police. Why did they have to be there, don't they have anything better to do, don't they know everyone is speeding, shouldn't they be chasing gang members or rapists? I was the one who was driving too fast, I knew what the speed limit was, I had the ability to control my speed and yet I chose to ignore all of the above and let my pride, my ego take over the responsibilities of driving. Why should I have to drive the speed limit, it is too slow, we all know that, it is unfair, just another way to tax us, a revenue source which has nothing to do with safety. Oh, how offensive we become when we are building our own defenses. I hate to admit that the only one to blame for my ticket was me, I just hate it. I hate to admit that because I failed to transfer money into an account in a timely fashion

I get charged a fee for the overdraft. How lame is that, how could they do that to me, those greedy banks, couldn't they see the money was there in another account just waiting to be transferred. They are so stupid. The only one who was stupid was me. Always pointing the finger at someone else before I carefully examined the reason I landed in a situation. We all do it.

We justify our actions regardless of how absurd or outrageous they are or what predicaments they get us into. Practicing perfection starts with our smallest acts. Put the cap back on the toothpaste. Put the milk back in the refrigerator. God is perfection, we are his creations and we are, all of us, capable of perfection and when that perfection is reached by all of us then we will have created a perfect world, a heaven on earth. I always had a fondness for the Zen approach which was when the monk asked the Master what the meaning of life was he answered, chop the wood and carry the water. In other words pay attention to the details of your everyday life because that is where God resides. He is there in front of you wherever you look waiting for you to notice him. So put out the trash, do the work assigned to you and pay attention to the life which is unfolding in front of you each day, every day.

Take a walk and look around you. The life which crashes against the beach of your world is God in all his glory. The movement, the faces, the falling leaves, the chill wind and each individual regardless of religion, race, sex, height, weight, intelligence, or any other identifying trait which you could imagine are manifestations of God. It can be no other way. There is undeniably a source of life without which we would not exist. It is undeniable that we all arise from that source and it nourishes us and sustains us until we die. It is the source of all energy and it is inexhaustible. This is what we refer to when we refer to God when we look for him in churches, our homes, our fields and into the sky. We are him and he is us the only difference is he has the big picture and we don't. He has the power of all life at his fingertips and we have the power within us to use as we decide. Our job is to find our own perfection for when we find that we will find God for God is in the details, in the moment. He can be no other place because he is not a memory, for his is constantly creating and a memory is a recorded moment in time not a present moment, the only moment where creation can actually take place.

There are literally millions of miracles taking place everyday right in front of our noses. We miss them when we are not paying attention, when we take personal credit for them we diminish them, we assume powers which we do not possess. Is it really so bad to not be all powerful? Is it so terrible to ask for help, to seek assistance with life's many difficulties? It is if you are afraid. Fear is held in abeyance by our fictional world of total control and power. We are only visitors here. We do not control very much, certainly not the most important issues in life. It is very scary to think that our powers are so limited, so inconsequential in the end. It is like being a helpless child again but this time there is no parent to turn to for comfort for support unless you have faith that there is a higher power who is accessible to man. The power we have chosen to call God. He is yours for the asking but you must leave your baggage behind. You can only find him in surrender. He will not court you, you must ask for him on your knees in all humility with an open heart and an open mind. Yield to the cosmic deity and the gates of heaven swing open for you with God smiling at you as if you were his long lost child returning home from a long and tortuous trip.

WHAT DO YOU

THINK?

POSTSCRIPT

God is not a copout. God is not a crutch, not an excuse, not a myth, not an invention of mankind, not a figment of our imagination, not a good fairy living in heaven, not an impotent fool blundering from house of worship to cathedral and not a captive of man. He is also beyond knowledge, beyond sight, beyond comprehension, beyond description. He is however, palpable, responsive, controlling, just, fair, accountable, responsible, reliable, available, understanding, infinite, cosmically intelligent, mysterious, profound, simple, magnetic, addictive, compelling, compassionate, objective, and wiser than we could ever imagine. God is worth the time and effort expended in searching for and finding him no matter how long it takes. God cannot be fooled or tricked or compelled or forced or managed or directed or scolded or damned. He does not register such human foibles. He knows the human heart, spirit and soul. He knows when they are out of harmony with the cosmic heart, spirit and soul. At the end of our individual lives we have all either made the choice to seek this thing we call God or we have not and at that endpoint, depending on our choice, we have closed the last chapter of our own book of life which has either been exalted by the presence of God in it or it has not.

When young David faced the giant Goliath on the battlefield with his simple sling he did the only wise thing that he could do. He looked to God and did not fear Goliath knowing that God would take care of the giant if he took care of the sling. The day he slew the Giant he did so with a pure faith, a bold heart and a full sling. Our task in this life is to go forward as David did into the unknown, the wilderness, leading with our faith, leaving our fears behind and being carried by the boldness of in our hearts. A stone rests neatly in our sling and we have attended to all the details. When we do this we are crossing the Red Sea that parted for the Israelites, fording the Jordan in the Spring when the flood waters were at full crest and slaying the Giant with our small stone and simple sling. Let God take care of the giants while we make sure we have stones for our sling. May God Bless us all.

The Interlude